Prophesying Daughters

Prophesying Daughters

BLACK
WOMEN
PREACHERS
AND THE
WORD,
1823–1913

Revised Edition

CHANTA M. HAYWOOD

University of Missouri Press | Columbia

Copyright © 2003 by
The Curators of the University of Missouri
University of Missouri Press, Columbia, Missouri 65211
Printed and bound in the United States of America
All rights reserved
First paperback printing, 2016

Library of Congress Cataloging-in-Publication Data

Haywood, Chanta M., 1968–
    Prophesying daughters : Black women preachers and the Word,
    1823–1913 / Chanta M. Haywood.
        p.   cm.
Includes bibliographical references and index.
    ISBN 978-0-8262-2070-7 (alk. paper)
    1. African American women clergy—History—19th century.
2. African American women clergy—History—20th century.
3. Prophecy—Christianity—History.   I. Title.
BR563.N4 H39 2003
251'.0082'0973—dc21   2003000562

Designer: Jennifer Cropp
Typefaces: Minion, Perseus, Flareserif

Jacket and frontispiece illustrations by Troy Tribble.

To my mother, Mary Jo Haywood
The wind beneath my wings

For my children
Jordan, Logan, and Kalen Roberts

And in loving memory of
Christy Haywood and Anna Faye Vaughn-Cooke

Contents

Preface

When I first read *Spiritual Narratives,* a collection of autobiographies of nineteenth-century black religious women published by Oxford University Press in 1988 (part of the Schomburg Library of Nineteenth-Century Black Women Writers), I experienced a dilemma. It stemmed from my dual religious upbringing in the South. My mother was a Baptist, my father was a Pentecostal minister, and I participated fully in both churches. Although trying to negotiate the distinct differences in doctrines and styles of both denominations made me experience a kind of religious dissociative disorder, one common denominator presented no conflict: the churches' expectations of women. As a girl and young woman, I could sing in the choir, usher, teach Sunday school, and participate in youth ministries. It was not within my conceptual or actual reach, however, to even aspire to be a minister. My brother could, and he did, and he is a minister today. Any preaching impulses that I or other women may have thought we had either were suppressed by negative, dissuading commentary made about other women who were "calling themselves preaching," or they were rechanneled into acceptable "female" positions such as choir director or Sunday school teacher.

Thus, when I first read the autobiographical narratives of Jarena Lee, Maria Stewart, Julia Foote, and Frances Joseph Gaudet, my discomfort was overwhelming on several levels. First, these women were all professing to be specifically called by God to preach and spread His word. I had been taught that women do not belong in the pulpit—that a woman's place was in the pews. Even when women spoke at different events at either one of my churches, they delivered their messages from a podium placed on the side of the pulpit. Although this practice has gradually changed, rarely, when I was growing up, did women stand behind the pulpit to preach. And here were these women saying—over a century ago—that they had been singled out to do what they were not supposed to do, but they did it anyway.

My dilemma? Do I abhor them, ignore them, or adore them? The upbringing that informed my religious view of the world and my place in it told me that women were not to be preachers. Interestingly, my mother, a civil rights activist, political advisor, and writer, had taught me to challenge ideologies, practices, and systems that marginalized and oppressed any group of people. This was reinforced by my womanist and feminist theory classes at the University of California, San Diego, so by the time I read these narratives I had developed an internal radar and hemostat that detected and dissected exclusionary tendencies, even those that existed in my immediate realities and institutions. Consequently, I knew that these women should be lauded and applauded. I pretty much had to do what these women had done—I had to figure out a strategy that would allow me to negotiate the complex act of challenging aspects of my Christian faith without giving up on it completely.

After accepting this dilemma as a condition that would not necessarily be resolved but would be an ever-shifting state in and of itself, I embraced these narratives with great fervor and zeal. I digested them and decided that my angle as a literary scholar would be one that would allow these religious women and what they had written to be used not only as a means of detecting and deconstructing flaws in religious institutions but also as a mechanism for expanding the field of African American literary criticism.

This leads to another dilemma I encountered. The field of African American literary studies provided very little space for me to really explore the profound theoretical implications of texts like these. Very little attention had been given to the religious component and its influences on the literary strategies blacks had adapted to writing. *Prophesying Daughters* is my attempt to address these issues.

I could not have produced the project without the assistance, commitment, and support of many people and institutions. Even as I question the misinterpretation of God's intentions for women—and even the misuse of those interpretations—I still must thank God Himself for blessing me with the good mental, physical, and intellectual health needed to take on such an endeavor. I thank my mother, Mary Jo Haywood—my anchor. I know that your knees are scuffed from your passionately praying for me throughout this process and my whole life. You are the wind beneath my wings. No matter how high I advance in life, I will always look up to you. To my husband, Gary Roberts, I appreciate you for letting these women preachers become part of your life and for making completing this book one of your top priorities. I thank you— especially for adjusting to the redefined structure our family took as I pursued this project and my professional aspirations. I thank Frances Smith Foster for getting me started and for making me finish, and for providing me with an excellent example to follow. George Lipsitz, thank you so much for believing in me and the importance of my work. Christopher Okonkwo, thank you for carefully reading my chapters and offering engaging and insightful comments. Beverly and Michael Carter, you opened your hearts, your home to me. I cannot thank you enough. I would also like to thank my graduate assistants, Patricia Symonnette and Tara Lake, for doing a lot of the intense, meticulous, and high-quality work during the last leg of producing this book. You went far and beyond the call of duty in cross-checking my references. Susan Brady, thank you for the excellent job in providing comments and recommendations that significantly enhanced the quality of my manuscript. Anna F. Vaughn-Cooke, former graduate dean at Florida A&M University and provost at University of Maryland, Eastern Shore, thank you for providing the understanding and support that only a quintessential scholar and administrator can provide. You were committed to administrators continuing to produce scholarship, and your support of me performing that component of my appointment has been invaluable. May you rest in peace.

One thing I learned in both my churches is that there is high risk involved in mentioning names. A name inadvertently left out can be the cause of serious church politics. Smart ministers and other speakers, in anticipation of this potential conflict, would preface each public acknowledgment with the caveat: "Charge it to my mind and not my heart if I forget anyone." Following in that tradition as I acknowledge several other people who have provided spiritual and emotional support over the years, I say, if I have forgotten anyone, please "charge it to my mind and not my heart."

I received several fellowships and grants that supported my research and writing: the Mellon Foundation Research Fellow Grant; University of California Chancellor's Postdoctoral Fellowship; and the Florida State University Council on Research and Creative Activity Summer Grant. I am grateful for their generosity.

I know that in academic texts you can't do "shout outs," but if I could, I would give "shout outs" to all my supporters, especially all of my family and friends from Camilla, Georgia, and Lake Wales, Florida. Other anchors have been my father, Elder Alonzo Smith; my stepmother, Alice Smith; Kimberley Smith; Barbara Smith; Monifa Love; Ann DuCille; Emma Waters Dawson; William Jones; Kim Hester-Williams; Lauren Wilson; Janet Roberts; Rod Ferguson; Thandi Onami; Trevena Favors; Louis Pratt; Darryl and Carol Dickson-Carr; Carol Batker; Jerrilyn McGregory; Donna Nudd; Genyne Boston; Deirdre Brown; Dara Winfield; Andres Johnson; Bruce Meeks; and Jackie and Stephen Knight.

I'd like to add that in so many ways exploring these women's lives has changed mine. Chapter six, which deals with Frances Joseph Gaudet's prison reform efforts, hit very close to home for me. While I was writing this book, our family became a part of the prison system. I say "our family" because the incarceration of one family member affects everyone. Each loved one suffers daily through this process: the expensive phone calls, the searches and screenings during visits, the anguish of missing your relative. I have come to realize that the more things have changed, the more they have remained the same. In the 1800s, Gaudet was speaking out against the disproportionate number of blacks in prison and the blatant double standards that exist in America's justice system. Angela Davis, my mother, and other activists have made the same observations and arguments. I dedicate that chapter to A.D. and the other men and women and families whose lives are impacted by this growing industry.

Finally, these women preachers have changed my life on a higher level. To use an Oprah term, they have allowed me to "remember my spirit." Their tenacity and even audacity have been inspiring and affirming. In the 1800s, they risked their lives and disrupted their families' routines by leaving for months in order to act out their unshakable belief that they had been called to change the world. Through transhistorical ministering, they taught me the importance of defining my own destiny and dreams and then being committed enough to myself to pursue and actualize them. As I mentioned earlier, I have made tremendous sacrifices that redefined my family structure. In chapter four, I discuss an idea I call prophetic journeying. It's about how travelling literally and metaphorically through life to carry out a divine purpose, or what Pablo Coehlo calls your "personal legend," you have to blur and challenge boundaries. Some people question it, but as did these women preachers, I continue to follow my calling. Finally, their lives also made me reflect upon the importance of acknowledging the spiritual presence of God in me and using it every day to make my segment of the world better. So, I thank Jarena Lee, Julia Foote, Maria Stewart, and Frances Gaudet for their legacy of spiritual and personal strength that I hope to pass on to my own children—Jordan, Logan, and Kalen—through my words, actions, and deeds.

Prophesying
Daughters

ONE

The Prophesying Daughters
BIOGRAPHICAL AND
HISTORICAL BACKGROUND

T hree times between 1804 and 1808 Jarena Lee, a young black maid,
contemplated killing herself.[1] First she was "tempted to destroy
[herself]" by drowning.[2] Her intention to carry out this act was diverted
just as she poised herself to jump into a "deep hole, where the water
whirled about among the rocks" (*Experience*, 5). Although this time her
"thoughts were taken entirely from this purpose," they reemerged four
years later, when she notes that she "was again tempted to destroy [her]
life by drowning" (*Experience*, 6). Again, inexplicably, she dismissed the
idea. Shortly after this second incident, Lee "was beset to hang [herself]
with a cord suspended from the wall enclosing the secluded spot" (*Experience*, 6). A young boy who was playing nearby distracted her, and
she abandoned the thought once again. Prior to each thought of suicide,
Jarena Lee had been to church and had felt an overwhelming sense of
religious conviction; she did not know exactly how or where to channel
the intense emotion it spurred.

Jarena Lee was born on February 11, 1783, in Cape May, New Jersey.
At the age of seven, she began work as a servant away from her poor
parents. Living during the aftermath of the Second Great Awakening,

1. In her autobiography, Jarena Lee does not reveal her family's last name. Consequently, she is referred to by her married name throughout this book.
2. Jarena Lee, *The Religious Experience and Journal of Mrs. Jarena Lee: Giving an
Account of Her Call to Preach the Gospel*, 4. Quotations from Lee's narrative are from
the 1988 Oxford University Press reprint edition. Hereafter citations of this work
will be made parenthetically, with the abbreviation *Experience* followed by the page
number.

she was surrounded daily by the religious fervor it aroused. She was also living in an era where women's experiences with religion and their roles for performing within religious contexts were clearly defined. Women usually served the church in some type of domestic position as members of the congregation, benevolent aid organizers, or Sunday school teachers. Blacks were considered spiritually inferior and often were described as not even having souls. Thus, the first time that "a ray of renewed conviction darted into [her] soul," Lee had trouble negotiating feelings that obviously contradicted these views (*Experience,* 3). Suicide seemed the best way out. After she decided against it, she suppressed her strong religious convictions.

Months later, while attending another church service—this one presided over by Richard Allen, founder of the African Methodist Episcopal Church—Lee leaped to her feet and began to testify about how God had delivered her soul. She felt that she had the "power to exhort sinners, and to tell of the wonders and of the goodness of [God]" (*Experience,* 5). Shortly afterward, she thought of attempting suicide again. For quite some time, though, Lee continued to struggle internally about her religious conviction. This dilemma was partially resolved after a visit from a black man named William Scott, who introduced Lee to the notion of sanctification, which he described as the "progress of the soul from a state of darkness" (*Experience,* 9). Sanctification was thought of as a state of complete spiritual purification and perfection. Three months after Scott's visit, Lee felt that she had achieved sanctification, and about five years later, she was convinced that she had been called by God Himself to preach. Despite her own certainty—which was informed by visions and spiritual confirmations by God—Lee knew that in that day and age, no one would believe that she, a black woman, was called to preach the gospel. If anyone could provide some direction about how and where to channel such conviction, it would be the leader and founder of the church, Richard Allen. She met with him and impressed upon him her belief that God had called her to preach. His response was that their discipline, the African Methodist Episcopal Church, "did not call for women preachers" (*Experience,* 11). Lee admits that she felt relieved of this burden.

In 1811, she married Joseph Lee, a minister, and she moved with him to Snow Hill, Maryland, where he had a church. For six years, Lee still experienced dreams and visions, which she interpreted as reinforcement of her call by God. Unfortunately, during the course of just three years,

Lee lost five close family members to death, including her husband. She was widowed with two children, and one of them was very sickly. A few years after her husband's death, Lee felt as if her call to preach was renewed, and she reapplied to Allen to be allowed to hold prayer meetings and to exhort; this time, she was granted permission.

Despite doctrinal rules and regulations prohibiting her from preaching, Lee never could shake the feeling that she had to do more than just hold prayer meetings and teach Sunday school. This feeling became a torrent while she was listening to a sermon being given by a minister who, by her own account, "seemed to have lost the spirit" (*Experience,* 17). With what she described as a "supernatural impulse" surging in her, she interrupted the preacher's sermon and began to expound upon his text (*Experience,* 17). Fearing expulsion from the church for such bold actions, Lee was surprised to learn that Allen considered her actions sufficient evidence that she was indeed called to preach. He granted her permission to preach, and she did so, but not without difficulty.

From that point on, Lee began traveling "up and down the world (to) promulgate the gospel of Christ" (*Experience,* 30). She preached in various towns in New Jersey, Pennsylvania, Delaware, Maryland, and New York. She left her children in the care of family members and friends. She visited and prayed for the sick in their homes, and she preached in private homes, churches, and bush clearings.

Lee apparently knew that what she was doing as a woman preacher was significant and unprecedented, because, despite the fact that she was not very educated, she began recording her life and travels. Fully aware of the power of the printed word, she also felt that by publishing a record of her work, she could proselytize to more people. In 1833, she decided to pay five dollars to have a portion of it published. She felt that her autobiographical sketch would be an "exercise to a dying world" (*Experience,* 66). In 1835, with the encouragement of friends and church members, Lee published a book. She was able to sell it in various cities, and she used the proceeds to pay for her living and travel expenses. Around 1849, with her texts selling well, Lee was encouraged to print a second edition at her own expense. She was over fifty years old when this issue was published. Many of her activities from this point are unknown.[3]

---

3. This biographical sketch was compiled using the following sources: Lee, *The Religious Experience and Journal of Mrs. Jarena Lee;* William Andrews, *Sisters of the*

In 1804, the year that Jarena Lee pinpoints as the beginning of her strong religious inclinations, a little girl named Maria Miller was barely one year old. She was born in Hartford, Connecticut, to free parents, both of whom had died by the time Maria was five years old. According to her, after she was orphaned, she was "bound out in a clergyman's family."[4] She provides very little information about this family but does acknowledge that it was while living with them that she had "the seeds of piety and virtue early sown in my mind" (*Productions*, 3). Like many free blacks in the North, Stewart notes that she was "deprived of the advantages of education, though [her] soul thirsted for knowledge" (*Productions*, 3). She lived with the minister's family until she was fifteen and attended Sabbath schools until she was twenty. She quite possibly worked as a domestic servant during this time.

In 1826, Maria Miller married James W. Stewart, described by her as a "tolerably stout, well-built man; a light, bright mulatto and about 30 years old."[5] James Stewart had made a fairly comfortable living as a "shipping master," or "shipping agent," fitting whaling and fishing vessels in Boston. In 1829, her husband became seriously ill, and he died on December 17. The following passage from a meditation published in a pamphlet (*Meditations from the Pen of Maria W. Stewart*, 1832) poignantly describes Maria's anguish over her husband's death: "O God, was not my conscience stung with remorse and horror, was not my soul torn with anguish, and did not my heart bleed when the summons came: 'He must die, and not live'" (*Productions*, 40). As heartrending

---

Spirit: Three Black Women's Autobiographies of the Nineteenth Century; and Jualyne Dodson's "Nineteenth-Century A.M.E. Preaching Women: Cutting Edge of Women's Inclusion in Church Polity."

It is important to note that Lee published only a portion of her journal. She noted that had she published it in its entirety, it would "probably make a volume of 200 pages; which, if the Lord willing, may at some future day be published" (*Experience*, 97). Lee's complete journal to date has not been published. Perhaps more research will lead to the publication of the entire journal, which would indeed reveal even more about her thoughts and her complicated life.

4. Maria Stewart, *The Productions of Mrs. Maria Stewart*, 3. Quotations from Stewart's work are from the 1988 Oxford University Press reprint edition. Hereafter citations of this work will be made parenthetically, with the abbreviation *Productions* followed by the page number.

5. Marilyn Richardson, *Maria Stewart, America's First Black Woman Political Writer: Essays and Speeches*, 117.

as her grief was, there is perhaps nothing more piercing than the fact that she was robbed of the sizable inheritance her husband left her. After two years of legal battles, shrewd white businessmen underhandedly deceived her of her inheritance.

Another life-altering year for Stewart came in 1830. First, she notes that she was "brought to the knowledge of the truth as it is in Jesus" (*Productions*, 4). She devoted her life not just to Christ but to the uplift of her race through Christ. She compellingly states: "From the moment I experienced the change, I felt a strong desire, with the help and assistance of God, to devote the remainder of my days to piety and virtue, and now possess that spirit of independence, that, were I called upon, I would willingly sacrifice my life for the cause of God and my brethren" (*Productions*, 4).

Her choice to be a martyr for her people through Christ is no coincidence. The same year that she received and accepted her call to elevate the race through Christ, a militant and outspoken political activist named David Walker mysteriously died. The year before (1829), Walker had produced the controversial pamphlet *Walker's Appeal, in Four Articles; Together with a Preamble, To the Coloured Citizens of the World, But in Particular, and Very Expressly, to Those of the United States Of America.* So fiery was Walker's manifesto that a hit had been placed on him. He was wanted dead or alive. One year later, he died of a cause that to this day has not been determined, although many suspect poison. David Walker was a very close, dear friend and mentor of Maria Stewart. She was devastated by his death.

Perhaps this at least partially explains Stewart's activism after his death. In 1831, she published her first essay, *Religion and the Pure Principles of Morality, The Sure Foundation on Which We Must Build*, in William Lloyd Garrison's abolitionist newspaper, The Liberator. Directed to a black audience, this essay was written, according to Stewart, "to arouse you to exertion, and to enforce upon your minds the great necessity of turning your attention to knowledge and improvement" (*Productions*, 3). She even references Walker and aligns herself with his martyrdom:

> Many will suffer for pleading the cause of oppressed Africa, and I shall glory in being one of her martyrs; for I am firmly persuaded, that the God in whom I trust is able to protect me from the rage and malice of

mine enemies, and from them that will rise up against me; and if there is no other way for me to escape, he is able to take me to himself, as he did the most noble, fearless, and undaunted David Walker.

The next year, Stewart "revolutionized prolific speaking" when she became the first woman, black or white, to address an audience of both men and women on political and social issues.[6] In September 1832, she lectured at an event sponsored by the Afric American Female Literary Society in Boston and spoke out against colonizing blacks to Africa. Between 1832 and 1833, she delivered four public speeches in which she addressed—in addition to the colonization issue—such pressing topics as poverty and oppression; education; the uplift of the race; securing a future for black children; and the role of women in black liberation.

Her audacity and tenacity incensed many of her community members, who found it difficult to accept a woman not only speaking publicly about political issues but also professing direction by God. Because of this public reaction, Stewart left Boston in 1832, never to see many of her friends and acquaintances there for nearly fifty years. After leaving Boston, she moved to New York and taught school there for several years. She quite possibly crossed paths with Jarena Lee, who was visiting and preaching in New York during this time.

Stewart later moved to Baltimore and then, during the Civil War, to Washington D.C. In Washington, she secured the position of matron of the Freedmen's Hospital, and while working there, Stewart learned of a pension law that entitled wives of veterans of the War of 1812 to a sizable claim. After securing all of the documentation necessary to prove that she was married to James Stewart and that he had indeed fought in the war, she was able to receive the pension. In 1879, she used the money to publish a new edition of her collected works.[7]

In 1823, just three years before Stewart married, a black girl named Julia Foote was born in Schenectady, New York, to very poor parents.[8]

---

6. Ida Young, "Keeping Truth on My Side: Maria Stewart," 117.

7. The information used in this biographical sketch was taken from Stewart, *The Productions of Mrs. Maria Stewart*; Richardson, *Maria Stewart, America's First Woman Political Writer*; and Young, "Keeping Truth on My Side."

8. As was the case with Jarena Lee, Julia Foote does not provide her family's last name in her descriptions of her early life. Her married name is being used throughout this book.

Her father, though born free, had been stolen as a child, enslaved, and forced to live a hard life of transporting merchandise and goods in severe weather. Foote's mother was born a slave in New York to a cruel master and mistress. On one occasion, according to Foote, her mother was severely beaten by her master for refusing his sexual advances. He gave her several lashes to her back, washed it with strong salt water, and let a week pass so that the clothes could stick to her back. The mistress jerked the clothing from her back, removing the skin and leaving her back raw and sore. Her mother was then sold from master to master. Eventually, her father was able to purchase himself, his wife, and their first child.

Foote's parents eventually joined the Methodist Episcopal Church, where they "were not treated as Christian believers, but as poor lepers."[9] While attending a service one day, Foote's mother and another black woman approached the communion table. They had been seated in the balcony, an area reserved for blacks only. Once they reached the lower door, two poor whites approached the table. The black women were admonished for not allowing even "the lowest of whites" to be served first (Brand, 11).

Although her parents attended and participated in church and "continued to attend the ordinances of God as instructed," Foote notes that they still kept liquor in the house (*Brand*, 12). Drinking liquor, she noted, was customary at funerals and weddings, and on occasion even the children were given the "bottom of the cup where the sugar and a little of the liquor was left, on purpose for them" (*Brand*, 12). Foote recalls that at around the age of five, she gained access to the chest where the liquor bottle was stored. She opened the bottle, "took it to [her] mouth and drained it to the bottom," nearly dying as a result (*Brand*, 12). She felt that God spared her life.

Foote recounts having religious inclinations as early as age eight, and she began reading from the Bible. Her father, though limited himself in education, taught her the alphabet from the Bible, since there were no schools that allowed black children admission. At age ten, she was sent to

---

9. Julia Foote, *A Brand Plucked from the Fire: An Autobiographical Sketch,* 11. Quotations from Julia Foote's text are from the 1988 Oxford University Press reprint edition. Hereafter citations of this work will be made parenthetically, with the abbreviation *Brand* followed by the page number.

live with "an old and influential family," who became quite fond of her because they had no children (*Brand,* 19). They sent Foote to school, where she witnessed the hanging death of her first teacher, Mr. Van Paten. He had murdered his fiancée's best friend for speaking out against their marriage, stating that she felt that Van Paten "was not very smart, and she did not see why this young lady should wish to marry him" (*Brand,* 21). Angered by this insult, the teacher went to the woman's house, killed her in front of her five children, and then told her husband what he had done. They hung him in front of the entire community. This event had a lasting impact on Julia's life, leading her later to speak out against capital punishment.

When a teenager, Foote returned home to help care for four younger siblings. She sometimes sneaked away from the house to attend parties and the theater. After attempting to dance at a quilting party, she fell to the floor and was unable to move for quite some time, feeling that God stopped her from dancing. Shortly after this incident, she was converted at age fifteen, and like Lee, she experienced internal conflicts about this. She continued to study from the Bible, and her drive for an education strengthened. She managed to save money to attend a school that eventually opened for colored children. The white family that operated the school had already suffered vicious attacks by a proslavery mob on a school they had operated previously. Weeks after opening the school that Foote attended, they closed and left town, forcing Foote to delay her education and continue studying from the Bible.

When Foote later felt compelled to be sanctified, her parents and other church members told her that sanctification was for the old. Against her mother's wishes, she received a visitor preaching sanctification, and under the visitor's instruction, she achieved this state of spiritual perfection. Later, a minister confronted her, telling her that many church members were "dissatisfied" with her actions—that she was too young to be acting the way that she was. Despite their disapproval, Foote continued to ground herself in religion.

At around the age of eighteen, she married a sailor named George Foote, despite her reservations about his not being sanctified. They moved to Boston, where she continued to encourage people to be sanctified. Her husband became disturbed by her following and her teaching, and eventually he went as far as to tell her that if she did not cease her activity, he was going to have her committed to an insane asylum. Later her husband went to sea for six months, and while he was away, Foote began visiting the sick and poor. During one of these visitations, she was reunited with a brother who had left their home at age seven.

Months later, Foote received her call from God to preach. Because of fear, she—like Lee—denied her calling. Foote herself was previously "opposed to the preaching of women" (*Brand*, 67). After continual internal conflicts, dreams, and visions, however, she accepted her call and was confronted with opposition from church members. Not only was she threatened with excommunication from the church, but those church members who listened to her also ran the risk of being expelled as well. To avoid such problems, Julia Foote began having meetings in private homes and halls. She appealed to the church conference to admonish a minister for his illegal attempt to excommunicate her, but her appeal was "slightingly noticed, and then thrown under the table" (*Brand*, 76). Of this repudiation, Foote—appropriating language used in the *Dred Scott* decision—commented that "even ministers of Christ did not feel that women had any rights which they were bound to respect" (*Brand*, 76).

Foote and other female conference attendees who either felt called to preach or who supported her secured a place to hold a meeting of their own, one that was "under the sole charge of women" (*Brand*, 83). Of course, they were confronted with resistance and were accused of trying to start their own conference. Foote denied the charges.

Such opposition did not stop Foote from continuing to travel and preach. She learned of her husband's death while preaching in Ohio. She resumed her travels and meetings almost immediately after taking care of the funeral arrangements. She traveled to places like New York, Ohio, Pennsylvania, Canada, and Baltimore. Again, it is quite possible that Foote crossed the paths of Lee and Stewart during this time. Almost fifty years after Jarena Lee's second edition was published, Julia Foote published her autobiography "to promote the cause of holiness in the Church" (*Brand*, 124). Foote's activities over the next twenty-five years are unknown.[10]

In 1861, when Julia Foote was at the height of her career as a preacher, Frances Joseph was born in Holmesville, Pike County, Mississippi, on

---

10. Foote's biographical sketch was compiled using information from Foote, *A Brand Plucked from the Fire;* and Andrews, *Sisters of the Spirit.*

November 25. She lived with her maternal grandparents until she was eight years old. Her grandfather, an A.M.E. preacher, was born a slave, and her grandmother—after whom she was named—was Native American. She had a very close relationship with her grandfather, who helped build one of the first churches for blacks in Summit, Mississippi. This school later became the first school for black children in that area, which Joseph attended. Their living conditions were so poor that often Gaudet and her brother would go barefoot in the summer to save their shoes for the winter.

When she was around eight years old, Joseph and her family fled to New Orleans after her uncle killed an overseer for making sexual advances toward his wife. Her uncle's fugitive status troubled her grandfather, who decided that it was best for the family to move. Frances and her brother were able to attend school in New Orleans. Unfortunately, while she was in the fourth grade, her grandparents died, leaving them with their mother and stepfather. Her mother sent her to Straight University, but upon her stepfather's death, Frances had to quit school and work to help support the household. She married at age eighteen and had three children, but she was legally separated from her husband ten years later because of his alcoholism. Shortly after her separation from her husband, she was called by God to serve Him.

Her call, she felt, was to be geared toward a particular population. In 1894, while praying for a distraught mother whose only child had been imprisoned, Gaudet stated that she received a demand from God to "go to the prison and ask the prisoners to pray that God will help them resist temptation; and ask them never to do anything to bring them back to the prisons when they get out of their present trouble."[11] After several weeks of visits to prisons, Gaudet was disturbed by the conditions of the prisons themselves, as well as by the moral and spiritual conditions of the prisoners and the prison workers. Determined to change these conditions, Gaudet became "the first American woman to choose mission work among Negro prisoners" (*Leadeth*, 2). She wrote letters for prisoners, secured food and clothing for them, provided moral and

11. Frances Joseph Gaudet, *He Leadeth Me,* 13–14. Quotations from Gaudet's narrative are from the 1996 Oxford University Press reprint edition. Hereafter citations of this work will be made parenthetically, with the abbreviation *Leadeth* followed by the page number.

mental support, and where she could, she defended them before judges and lawyers.

She extended her services beyond the prisoners to help abandoned or orphaned young people, often keeping children in her home, teaching them self-help skills and giving them moral instruction. In 1902, after traveling all over the country to secure funds, she founded the Colored Industrial Home for Boys and Girls. Modeled after Booker T. Washington's Tuskegee Institute, the Home focused on giving children and teenagers vocational and agricultural training and teaching them moral and religious values. They were instructed also in farming, cooking, sewing, and carpentry as well as business skills.

Gaudet continued to travel nationally and internationally, spreading the Word of God and securing funds for her school. In 1913, with the encouragement of her friends, she published her autobiography, *He Leadeth Me*.[12]

When situated within the general context of free black life in the nineteenth century, Jarena Lee, Maria Stewart, Julia Foote, and Frances Joseph Gaudet were, in fact, like many of their black contemporaries. They struggled daily financially and politically. With slavery still at its height in the South, laws were being passed to confound black life even more. The Fugitive Slave Act of 1850 made it more difficult for slaves to escape, providing for the return of escaped slaves to their masters and making it a federal crime for any person, white or black, to aid in the escape of slaves. The Compromise of 1850 added strength to the Fugitive Slave Act by stipulating that federal officials were to return escaped slaves, and the officials' cooperation was made enticing by offering rewards for apprehending slaves.

Furthermore, in the *Dred Scott v Sanford* case, the U.S. Supreme Court ruled in 1857 that blacks were not citizens. The court concluded that Scott could not sue for his freedom in a free state because of his status

---

12. Gaudet's work and religious activities will be discussed in greater detail in chapter six. This biographical sketch of Gaudet was compiled using the following sources: Chanta Haywood, introduction to *He Leadeth Me,* by Frances Joseph Gaudet; Violet H. Bryan, "Frances Joseph Gaudet: Black Philanthropist"; Frank Lincoln Mather, ed., *Who's Who in the Colored Race: A General Biographical Dictionary of Men and Women of African Descent;* and A. E. Perkins, ed., *Who's Who in Colored Louisiana: Brief Sketches of History and Biography.*

as property, for as chattel, he had "no rights a white man was bound to respect."

In the North, free blacks like Lee, Foote, and Stewart were still affected by the racist ideologies informing slavery and the laws surrounding it. Given the rewards associated with capturing slaves, free blacks constantly faced the possibility of being kidnapped and sold into slavery. Antiblack laws restricting and degrading blacks were also enacted. As a result of these "black laws," or "black codes," blacks were not granted citizenship and had to live in the worst neighborhoods, sit in balconies or "black sections" of churches and theaters, and ride in the baggage sections of trains and ships. That Foote's parents were publicly reprimanded for approaching the altar before even the poorer whites had prayed shows further evidence of the extremely precarious situations in which these religious women lived.

Like many of the other free black women during their times, these religious women's collective experiences show, as George Moses Horton has noted, that many black women helped their families make ends meet by working as domestic servants. As the lives of Lee, Foote, and Stewart reveal, young black girls left their parents to help them survive. If, when they were older, they became parents themselves, they left their children to work.

Collectively, these women's lives show that they also had to contend with restrictive gender expectations. Often their husbands opposed their activities. Male and some female parishioners openly challenged and protested against them. Male preachers were so outraged and incensed by their preaching and proselytizing that they vehemently enforced church policies prohibiting such activity.

In this sense, these women collectively would not appear particularly distinctive. Yet they were. They knew they were. They knew that their calls by God and their dedication to the call made them different—made them spiritual interrogators of the status quo. Feeling directed by God, they challenged gender restrictions. Fueled by their convictions, they questioned political and social wrongs. Inspired by and filled with a holy zeal, they set out to make changes where they could. In doing so, they left an impressive list of firsts: Jarena Lee was the first woman to be ordained in the African Methodist Episcopal Church; Maria Stewart was the first woman, black or white, to speak publicly about political issues to a diverse audience; Julia Foote was the first woman ordained a deacon in the A.M.E. Zion Church; and Frances Joseph Gaudet was the first woman, black or white, to conduct mission reform among black prisoners. The following chapters establish how as pioneers, these religious women ontologically situated religion and religious conviction at the center of African American women's literary history, meriting pause for a critical consideration of the serious implications of their views and writings to the field.

 TWO

The Act of Prophesying

NINETEENTH-CENTURY BLACK WOMEN
PREACHERS AND BLACK LITERARY HISTORY

"After this I shall pour out my spirit on all mankind: / your sons and your *daughters will prophesy.* . . . I shall pour out my spirit in those days even on slaves and slave-girls."

—Joel 2:28–29

The biblical passage above is used repeatedly in the narratives of Jarena Lee, Julia Foote, Maria Stewart, and Frances Joseph Gaudet. These women used this passage most frequently to convince skeptics and opposers that their religious activities were a part of God's will and to refute nineteenth-century gender and racial ideologies that suggested that women should not and could not preach or work in a capacity outside of domestic church positions. During the nineteenth century, women in the black church were relegated to positions that posed no real threat to the power structure maintained by preachers, deacons, and other male leaders. Women were usually assigned roles of Sunday school teachers, exhorters, secretaries, cooks, and cleaners. Such positions paralleled those reserved for women within the domestic sphere of the home. Although Evelyn Higginbotham has demonstrated the political roles that women played within the Baptist institution, and although Jualyne Dodson has intimated that women's financial contributions to the church gave them power in decision-making processes within the church, women were still expected to operate within gender guidelines that reflected the expectations for women in society at large. Those who dared to become preachers or even independent missionaries were often met with strong opposition by men and even

14

some women. In response, use of this passage declaring that God is "pouring out [His] spirit upon all flesh" offered justification that the Bible had already mandated spiritual egalitarianism in terms of who could prophesy. The Bible clearly states that the "sons and the daughters" could prophesy, yet within the particular historical context of these black women preachers, only the sons were being privileged.

As descendants of "slaves" or as former "slave girls" themselves, Jarena Lee, Julia Foote, Maria Stewart, and Frances Gaudet strongly believed that they were indeed these "prophesying daughters." As such, they traveled all over the country, sometimes even abroad, to preach or do God's work. Whenever possible, they rode on trains or in stagecoaches, but most of the time they were forced either to ride on the decks of boats and in mail coaches or to rely on other forms of transportation because of what Julia Foote calls "indignities on the account of color." Many times they walked. When they reached their destinations in free and slave states, they preached to men, women, and children from various races, denominations, and classes, extending to them their own interpretations of the Bible. When they were denied the pulpit or podium because of prejudices against women, they preached in tents, bush clearings, meeting halls, private homes, and other marginal spaces. They left their children, husbands, and homes to preach the Word of God.

Jarena Lee, Julia Foote, Maria Stewart, Frances Joseph Gaudet, and several other religious black women spread the Word of God to slaves in the South and to a very large number of diverse blacks in the North. Even within their own immediate black communities and institutions—in what scholars such as Carla Peterson call "ethnic public spheres"—and within nineteenth-century mainstream white society at large, the women confronted class, race, and gender ideologies shaped to make preaching or independent missionary work very difficult for them.[1] They confronted the domestic ideology that positioned them in the home and the racist ideology that positioned them as naturally inferior to whites. They faced laws and customs restricting blacks socially and physically as well as the socioeconomic reality that they, as blacks and women, were part of a large class of unskilled laborers. They continued to rebuke such limitations, however, by invoking their positions as God's

1. Carla Peterson, *Doers of the Word: African American Women Speakers and Writers in the North, 1830–1880,* 8.

prophesying daughters, who had been called to travel to bring the truth and Word of God as they saw it to the American and, in some cases, foreign public.

Perhaps the most significant fact about these "prophesying daughters" is that they had the insight and vision to record their experiences and philosophical views. As historical agents writing themselves into existence, they left stories of bold women who were steadfast and unmovable in their determination to live up to their call from God. I do not intend to privilege the technology of writing here or to suggest that these women did not exist unless or until they wrote or spoke in public. They are accessible to us—and may have been accessible to their audiences—through writing and speaking, but they already existed outside of writing and speaking. As writers, they charted an important part of African American literary history that was couched in terms of—and informed significantly by—their religious conviction. In fact, their writing was inspired by their religious conviction and was seen as a tool to further that conviction.

Fortunately, we can follow the trailblazing work of literary scholars such as Frances Smith Foster, William Andrews, Carla Peterson, and Joanne Braxton, among others, whose excellent work places black religious women's texts within the larger context of black women's writings.[2] In this study, I will show how the nineteenth-century struggle for a visible and viable public presence by black women preachers led to the creation of "prophetic" written texts and oral proclamations that deserve careful scrutiny in the present.

Work from scholars in religious and historical studies has also been extremely important in ensuring that the contributions of these prophesying daughters are not lost. Scholars such as Marilyn Richardson, Jualyne Dodson, Jean Humez, Bettye Collier-Thomas, and Evelyn Higginbotham have done thorough and groundbreaking work on black

---

2. See Frances Smith Foster, *Written by Herself: Literary Production by African American Women, 1746–1892;* Peterson, *Doers of the Word;* Joanne Braxton, *Black Women Writing Autobiography: A Tradition within a Tradition;* William Andrews, *To Tell a Free Story: The First Century of Afro-American Autobiography, 1760–1865;* and Andrews, introduction to his *Sisters of the Spirit.* Other literary scholars such as Dolan Hubbard, Maxine Montgomery, Kenny Williams, Hortense Spillers, and Chester Fontenot Jr. have contributed to our understanding of the relationship between theology, biblical style, and literary production.

religious women, highlighting their significant roles in religious and historical studies.[3] However, we have paid very little attention to how these women's prophesying influenced their literary strategies and approaches. Furthermore, an analysis of prophesying as a religious rhetoric and literary trope could lead to new possibilities for interpreting African American literature containing undercurrents of religion and religious rhetoric. Even more, little has been written that connects the idea of prophesying to the development of African American literary history in general and African American women's literary history in particular. Reading the idea of prophesying into African American literary and women's histories is imperative if we are to more fully appreciate the extent to which religious conviction compelled these women to speak and write truth as they saw it, even if it meant opposing national political leaders and leaders within their own race and congregation.

I define prophesying as the use of a perceived mandate from God to spread His word in order to advance a conscious or unconscious political agenda. My analysis of these women as prophesying daughters finds conceptual support in Cornel West's notion of "prophetic pragmatism," which, according to West, is a "universal consciousness that promotes an all-embracing democratic and libertarian moral vision, historical consciousness that acknowledges human finitude and conditionedness and a critical consciousness that encourages relentless critique and self-criticism for the aims of social change and personal humility."[4]

West notes that the act of prophetic pragmatism can be carried out in various political movements and within different religious or secular traditions. I am situating my study of nineteenth-century black women preachers' prophetic pragmatism within the Christian tradition in which these women understood and identified themselves. Because many black religious women referred to Joel 2:28–29 in order to assert themselves as prophesying daughters, they aligned themselves with

---

3. See Richardson, *Maria W. Stewart, America's First Black Woman Political Writer*; Dodson, "Nineteenth-Century A.M.E. Preaching Women"; Jean Humez, ed., *Gifts of Power: The Writings of Rebecca Jackson, Black Visionary, Shaker Eldress*; Evelyn Higginbotham, *Righteous Discontent: The Women's Movement in the Black Baptist Church, 1880–1920*; and Bettye Collier-Thomas, *Daughters of Thunder: Black Women Preachers and Their Sermons, 1850–1879*.

4. Cornel West, "On Prophetic Pragmatism," in *The Cornel West Reader*, 170.

prophets in the Christian tradition, who, according to West, "brought urgent and compassionate critique to bear on the evils of their day. The mark of the prophet is to speak the truth in love with courage come what may."[5] My use of the term *prophesying,* then, accords more with a God-inspired critical consciousness that intends to promote social change rather than with popular conceptions of prophesying as the possession of a visionary gift that allows one to see into or predict the future.

My analysis of prophesying from this perspective is akin—but not identical—to Mae Henderson's notion of "speaking in tongues," a theory she advances to account for the "simultaneity of discourse" present in the works of black women writers. Juxtaposing Bakhtin's model of dialogism and Gadamer's "dialectical model of conversation," Henderson explains that idea of simultaneity as the complex ability of black women writers to "speak a discourse of racial and gendered difference in the dominant and hegemonic discursive order" and to "speak a discourse of racial and gender difference in the subdominant discursive order."[6]

My project is similar to Henderson's in that the thrust of our theories incorporates and explores the religious domain of many black women's lives. Henderson goes to the Bible and genealogically situates her notion of speaking in tongues in Genesis 11; 1 Corinthians 14; and Acts. Genesis 11 reveals the futility—because of language barriers—of efforts to build a tower in the city of Babel. One Corinthians 14 implies man's ability to speak in tongues directly to God in a language understood between God and the communicant. Acts details how the disciples are filled with the Spirit and are able to speak the different languages, or tongues, of the various groups represented in crowds they were addressing. Each person was able to understand the disciples as if they were speaking in her/his own tongue. Each of these passages discusses the ability to communicate despite differences. Henderson likens the "polyphony, multivocality and plurality of voices that make up Black women's subjectivity" and the "intimate, private, and inspired utterances that make up their writing" to their unique ability to speak in tongues.[7]

5. Ibid, 171.
6. Mae Henderson, "Speaking in Tongues: Dialogics, Dialectics, and the Black Woman's Literary Tradition," 121.
7. Ibid.

My study departs from Henderson's in that I focus not on the idea of speaking in tongues but rather specifically on the concept of prophesying and its scriptural and literary possibilities. The Scriptures seem to see in prophesying a force for change in the statement in 1 Corinthians 14:4–6 that "He who speaks in a tongue edifies himself, but he who prophesies edifies the church. I wish you all spoke with tongues, but even more that you prophesied: for he who prophesies is greater than he who speaks with tongues, unless indeed he interprets, that the church may receive edification. But now brethren, if I come to you speaking with tongues, what shall I profit you unless I speak to you either by revelation, by knowledge, by prophesying or by teaching?" The implication here is that being able to bridge differences through language is important, but it is more imperative to be able to speak to diverse groups in a way that is not only understandable but also corrective. Although understanding sites of difference that compose black female identity is important, what is even more important is knowing how that difference is used to enact social change. Speaking in tongues requires that someone interpret what is being said; it carries with it a riddlelike quality. Prophesying, on the other hand, is not just about "difference" but also about justice; it is not just about interpreting text but also about understanding and furthering social change. Furthermore, the very act of writing is prophetic: the texts by the black women preachers under study were written, according to the writers, to "edify, change, and comfort." In defending her right to prophesy, Julia Foote, for example, points readers to the scripture that defines prophesying: "In the eleventh chapter of first Corinthians, Paul gives directions, to men and women, how they should appear when they prophesy; and he defines prophesying to be speaking to edification, exhortation and comfort" (*Brand,* 79).

Looking at prophesying from this perspective, I adhere to William Andrews's admonition that we "start asking as many questions about the formal dimensions of (autobiography) as we posed about its thematic dimension."[8] My aim, consequently, is to explore *how* this idea of prophesying plays itself out as a rhetorical literary device and as a political strategy for black women preachers of the nineteenth century. By claiming, on the rhetorical level, a God-mandated subjectivity when they sat

8. William L. Andrews, "Toward a Poetics of Afro-American Autobiography," 80.

down to write within a social context of reader distrust, sentimentality, and race and gender exclusion, the women were able to use markers of Christianity such as conversion, apostolic travel, and biblical interpretation in their writing to challenge sociological restrictions. On the level of sociopolitical strategy, this religious conviction became a cultural passport, allowing the women access to physical and ideological spaces otherwise denied them. Once inside these spaces, these women were able to use the gaps between the various systems of hierarchy to their own advantage: they used gender solidarity to challenge race exclusion, and racial solidarity to challenge gender exclusion. Because black women preachers interpreted one aspect of their negotiations with God as a call to travel and promulgate the Word, they presented a powerful challenge to dominant nineteenth-century ideas about woman's proper space. For example, they redefined the home from a discrete space bounded by four walls to a shifting zone that expanded with the geographical area they covered and the number of people they converted during their travels.[9]

Understanding the works of many nineteenth-century black writers from a perspective that emphasizes religious conviction, I recognize at the onset the need to address possible concerns about situating a discussion of black women preachers within masculinist contexts like the Bible and Christianity. It may seem contradictory to explore black women's prophesying when the world of Christian tradition in which the women preached and wrote was patriarchal and when the religious discourse of the nineteenth century privileged the masculine. Yet this paradox accounts for the main contribution made by these prophesying daughters to African American literary studies and to black feminist thought. Just as blacks were able to embrace Christianity despite its hegemonic use to justify enslaving and oppressing the race, black women preachers engaged in a similar critical endeavor. They were able to negotiate this seeming contradiction by engaging in what I call a discursive inversion of what traditional (masculine) religiosity and even creation mythology and other aspects of the biblical world present as the natural order of things. In other words, they flipped the religious script. This is indeed what Sojourner Truth does when she says: "Where

---

9. For more discussion of ways that black women use the margin as a site of resistance, see bell hooks's "Choosing the Margin as a Space of Radical Openness," in *Yearning: Race, Gender, and Cultural Politics.* Also, for a discussion on how slave narrators used marginality, see Andrews, *To Tell a Free Story.*

did your Christ come from? From God and a woman. Man had nothing to do with him." Truth then goes on to center Eve (woman), noting that, "if de fust woman God ever made was strong enough to turn de world upside down all her one lone, all dese togeder ought to be able to turn it back and get it right side up again, and now dey is asking to, and de men better let 'em."[10] Jarena Lee echoes Truth's sentiment by inverting masculinist religious discourse that forbids women preaching: "If man may preach because the Saviour died for him, why not the woman? seeing he died for her also. Is he not a whole Saviour, instead of a half one? as those who hold it wrong for a woman to preach, would seem to make it appear" (*Experience,* 11).

In *Prophesying Daughters,* I seek to identify the uniquely black contributions to the feminist tradition of inversion. The black women preachers are inverting what is perhaps the most masculine discourse of all—Christianity. The women I discuss in this book are prophets, on the one hand, in the sense in which Cornel West employs the term. On the other hand, in the particular ways in which they appropriated, inverted, and womanized "Father Law," they also became—or can be read today as—prophets of a new and enduring feminism.

Centering the idea of prophesying as a trope for God-inspired social critique, I engage several major concerns in this book. First is what I call an "institutionalized absence" of black women preachers' texts from African American literary studies and black feminist intellectual history. African American literary history in general and black feminist studies in particular have taken little note of the social, political, and literary ramifications of the intricacies and even contradictions present in black women's uses of religious conviction.

Some scholars, however, have situated individual women preachers splendidly within larger contexts of women's literary history. Frances Smith Foster's *Written by Herself,* for example, focuses on the politics of production and its impact on black women writers. She studies Jarena Lee within the general context of writers like Harper, Keckley, and others. Carla Peterson, in *Doers of the Word,* analyzes black writers, speakers, and activists who were actively challenging dominant ideologies and insisting on their rights to speak publicly and to write on various political

---

10. Nell Irvin Painter, *Sojourner Truth: A Life, A Symbol,* 168.

issues that affected them. In this context, she places women preachers Jarena Lee and Maria Stewart alongside other prominent black women writers and activists such as Mary Ann Shadd Cary, Nancy Prince, Frances Harper, and Harriet Wilson. Joanne Braxton, in *Black Women Writing Autobiography,* places these women within the larger tradition of black women writing autobiography. Similarly, William Andrews's *To Tell a Free Story* places Jarena Lee within a larger black autobiographical tradition. Although his *Sisters of the Spirit*—which introduces three autobiographies by black women preachers—does begin to view their works collectively, it does not provide a thorough consideration of their texts. The centrality of prophesying to black women's literary works has not yet been fully explored.

This critical lapse is due in part to our tendency, since the Black Arts movement, to see the acceptance of Christianity by earlier generations of blacks as assimilationist and retrograde. "For disciples of the Black Arts Movement, early African-American literature was an embarrassment or 'Exhibit A' that proved misguided or appropriated genius."[11] This valuing of the role of Christianity in African American literature is ahistorical, however. Though Christianity was used as a tool to justify oppressing blacks in the nineteenth century, it was also employed by blacks themselves as an instrument of spiritual and literal liberation. Nowhere is this more evident than in the revolutionary actions and views of Nat Turner and Gabriel Prosser, whose interpretations of Christianity led to their revolts and insurrections.[12] Christian ethics and ideologies abound in eighteenth- and nineteenth-century African American literature, as exemplified in the works of Phillis Wheatley, Jupiter Hammon, and Frances E. W. Harper. Their works reflect that many African Americans accepted Christianity and used it in their own ways, sometimes creating their own theological approaches. The paucity of discussion of this issue by literary scholars has contributed to the limited number of theories we have that explore how the religious belief systems of African Americans informed how and what they wrote.

11. Frances Foster and Chanta M. Haywood, "Christian Recordings: Afro-Protestantism, Its Press, and the Production of African American Literature," 17.

12. For an excellent discussion of literary responses to Nat Turner, see Mary Kemp Davis, *Nat Turner before the Bar of Judgment: Fictional Treatments of the Southampton Slave Insurrection.*

Closely related to the downplaying of the seriousness and influence of religion on literary strategies of black women writers is the subscription by some scholars to the Marxist view that religion is the opiate of the masses. Many scholars are uneasy with the seeming contradiction contained in the fact that early African American writers accepted and believed in a Christian religious ideology used to justify the oppression of blacks and women. Similarly, the appearance that many blacks believe so strongly in the promise of a rich and glorious afterlife, that they seem complacent with their condition on Earth, and that they are not inclined to protest because of a belief that God is good all the time despite their harsh conditions does not set too well with some scholars. This discomfort with dealing with religion in literary circles makes it easier to just leave such issues up to our colleagues in religious studies, divinity schools, and seminaries.[13] If religion is indeed an opiate, as Marx suggests, and if it is an anesthetizing agent, then how can we account for the religious sentiment that propelled Nat Turner's revolt or the radical religiosity that informed David Walker's *Appeal*? Moreover, how do we explain the *Christian Recorder* being banned from the South because of its strong political essays on the same page that featured moral lessons?[14]

The *Recorder* really did not distinguish itself from other secular newspapers. The issues it addressed were just as politically charged, explaining why slaveholders observed it closely. That this religious newspaper was also secular in its politics calls for the deconstruction of the secular/religious binary that exists in African American literary studies. Within the discipline, there has been a tendency to privilege secular

---

13. In fact, while at the College Language Association Conference in 1995, I was asked, after giving a paper on this very issue, why it is that I don't just let the people in religious studies handle this topic.

14. Deemed the "official organ" of the African Methodist Episcopal Church, the *Christian Recorder* was started by Richard Allen and other church founders to provide a forum for black leadership and education. Though founded and produced by the church, the *Recorder* confronted and engaged with political issues of the day. In *The Early Black Press in America, 1827–1860,* Frankie Hutton notes that in addition to dispensing moral advice, the *Recorder* offered writing with social and political themes that "parallel those of the secular papers" (xvi). Frederick Detweiler also informs us in *The Negro Press in the United States* that "this paper was looked upon by the slave holders of the South and the pro-slavery people of the North as a very dangerous document or sheet and was watched with a critical eye. It could not be circulated in the slave states" (43).

material over the religious, dismissing the religious as assimilationist, retrograde, or just not as serious. What has resulted is what I call an institutionalized absence of religious literature. The *Recorder* contains a preponderance of literature by nineteenth-century blacks. If such literature is dismissed because of its location and religious themes, then we may be overlooking a key aspect of African American literary expression that explores the interchangeability of the secular and the religious. The boundary between the two is not easily drawn.

The literature of black religious women reveals them using religious rhetoric and discourse as a protest against and a response to their situation as blacks and women in the nineteenth century. Jarena Lee's constant urging that her readers prepare themselves now for a glorious life in heaven shows that as Christians, she and her contemporaries believed in a life beyond their sojourn on Earth. But, on the other hand, when she entitles one of the chapters in her autobiography, "Indignities on the Account of Color," she also indicates that she—and implicitly other religious black women of her era—knew that the discrimination, disenfranchisement, and degradation that informed their conditions and realities were morally wrong. They used their calls as prophesying daughters not only to condemn those wrongs but also to offer alternatives. Their responses to injustice inform the themes, content, and even style of their literature.

This nuanced understanding of religion has rarely been circulated in black feminist thought. The primary reason seems to be our somewhat uncritical adherence to the modernist impulse to rid oneself of religion, to kill God, so to speak. Black feminist critics such as Frances Smith Foster, Carla Peterson, Hazel Carby, Claudia Tate, Deborah McDowell, Ann duCille, and others have rightly examined the cultural and political ramifications of black women's identities and expressions as sites of critical articulation and engagement. Although many critics of African American letters, including black women writers, have acknowledged the role of religious views in the literature, few of us have taken seriously enough the material significance of religion.[15]

In her excellent recent book on the spiritual narratives of nineteenth-century African American women, Joycelyn Moody offers an interesting

---

15. See Maxine Lavon Montgomery, *The Apocalypse in African American Fiction.*

explanation for the "anti-spiritual context in which early black women's writings are generally read." She speculates that perhaps this gap exists "in part because of African American feminist scholars' vexed relationship with the stereotype of the black church woman." This figure, Moody continues, "has been maligned in traditionally canonical literature and popular culture alike by African American critics as dissimilar as writers James Baldwin (in for example, the *Amen Corner* and *If Beale Street Could Talk*) and Toni Morrison (*The Bluest Eye*), and comedians Flip Wilson and Martin Lawrence."[16] In her study, Moody debunks such stereotypes and opens up a space, as I set out to do here, for a serious consideration of the theoretical significance of religious women's works.

This is not to suggest that we literary scholars who have yet to consider the serious importations of religion in literature should now run out and "get religion." I am suggesting only that, at this point in the development of the field, we not *forget* religion in our formulations of theories on how to read and understand black women's texts. Otherwise we will continue to overlook and even misread and misunderstand a large segment of our literature and religious history, both sacred and secular.

Society's privileging of the secular and scientific over the sacred contributes inherently to the dismissal of the religious component of black women's writings. If we allow space to consider the religious component of black women's writing strategies, then we will see how their works obfuscate the secular and religious dichotomies we have created in black feminist thought. The narratives of Jarena Lee, Julia Foote, Frances Gaudet, and Maria Stewart reveal that as prophesying daughters, they drew no lines between their religious ideologies and their political and social commitment. Frances Joseph Gaudet, for example, visited prisons not merely to preach to prisoners but even more to attempt to convert them and provide spiritual guidance. She notes that often "I have gone to them and urged them to repent their sins and resolve to live better lives" (*Leadeth*, 17). While going to the prisons, Gaudet saw that the conditions of the prisons were substandard, that deputies and guards brutally abused and mistreated the prisoners, that young offenders were placed in the same facilities with older, hardened criminals, and that many of the prisoners received unfair sentences.

16. Joycelyn Moody, *Sentimental Confessions: Spiritual Narratives of Nineteenth-Century African American Women*, xi, 176.

As for the prisoners' spiritual needs, Gaudet states, "My work has not stopped here" (*Leadeth,* 17). She felt a political obligation to the prisoners as well: "I have gone to the judge and pleaded for leniency. Some have had their sentences set aside, some have been kept from going to state prison, having their time spent in the city where they are better treated and where their friends can come to see them" (*Leadeth,* 17). Noting the political effect of her visits and presence as an advocate in the prisons and jails, Gaudet states further that "these visits to the prison cause the deputies to treat the prisoners better for the fear of being reported to higher officials has great force. I have had this to do more than once" (*Leadeth,* 17).

The secular/religious binary we have set up in the black feminist study of literature causes us to miss the fluidity between the mutually constitutive aspects of political and religious meanings. Gaudet, for example, could preach to the prisoners about their souls but still advocate for them and fight for their rights. Clearly, her political and religious missions intersected. As Bettye Collier-Thomas persuasively argues, women preachers in particular "struggled to follow God's call to preach, they taught by example as well as by their words how to negotiate the reality of what the world is with Christian vision of what the world should be."[17]

The women preachers' tendency to blur the secular and the religious stems in part from the dialogical nature of their works. As suggested in Bakhtin's notion of dialogism in language, all languages "may be juxtaposed to one another, mutually supplement one another, contradict one another and be interrelated dialogically. As such they encounter one another and co-exist."[18] Reflecting upon Bakhtin's argument, I call their works dialogic because the women's political and religious actions and writings were interrelated. Their views of themselves as prophesying daughters made it impossible for one to exist without the other. Gaudet's meeting with the judge to secure rights for the prisoners whom she is interested in converting exemplifies the coexistence of the secular and the religious. Because black religious women saw their actions as a part of the larger project of saving souls, they often ventured into various secular and religious spaces, speaking to Native American, white, and black male and female Presbyterians, Baptists, and

17. Collier-Thomas, *Daughters of Thunder,* 8.
18. M. M. Bakhtin, *The Dialogic Imagination,* 292.

Methodists in churches, city halls, and bush clearings. No space, religious or secular, was off limits to them.

Because of the dialogical nature of their work, because of their constant interaction with multiple audiences mixed by region, race, and class, and because they did not preach, live, and write in a vacuum, these women had to take a multivocal approach to speaking and writing. This unique subject position informs their discourse with a rich intersectional quality that is both fluid and fixed, determined and dynamic. Because this intersectionality is encoded in their texts, it is difficult for me to argue for an authentic, pure black female aesthetic. Nevertheless, I *still* feel the need to defend how crucial it is to situate these women's works and activity within the black feminist category. With the interest in and appropriation of black women's texts and theories by some men and by white feminist critics in particular, I can see how the previous assertion about the dialogic nature of these black religious women's works could be misinterpreted as a green light for authorizing some scholars to further appropriate their works. Ann duCille alerts us to the nature of this appropriation when she notes that "in the midst of this multicultural moment, the texts of black women have become politically correct, intellectually popular, and commercially precious." White feminist and some black male scholars who have benefited from black women's works (by way of publications and career enhancement) have read those works in ways that are informed by their own agendas and do not acknowledge the tradition of scholars responsible for unearthing and then analyzing their works in the first place. Black women's lives and texts have therefore become, duCille continues, "an-any-body-can-play pick up game played on an open field."[19] So while I acknowledge the multiplicitous nature of black women preachers' and missionaries' own activity, I still assert that their works be seen as black feminist. I do so in order that the particular character of their texts informed by being black and women is not subsumed under the larger category of woman or dismissed because they are departed daughters who are airing dirty laundry within black religious institutions.

I argue for situating the works of black women preachers and missionaries within black feminist paradigms because, regardless of how inclusive these women preachers were in their own philosophies or views,

19. Anne duCille, *Skin Trade,* 84.

they somehow have been excluded from literary and political histories. It is this very exclusion that has made it necessary for scholars and critics who study their lives to create a critical space for them to even be considered. For example, the degree of cultural exchange reflected in the works of these black women preachers is not reflected in other forms of dominant discourse, particularly white women's religious politics. Early in the nineteenth century, white feminists argued for more visibility of women in the pulpit, and many of these same women were actively involved in social issues such as suffrage, temperance, and the abolition of slavery. Religious feminists such as Elizabeth Cady Stanton and Sarah and Angelina Grimke were quick to make the connection between religion and the social and political oppression of women. Elizabeth Cady Stanton and Susan B. Anthony were primary proponents of women having higher religious positions. They both asserted that the "moral" and "religious" reasons used to support the subordinate roles prescribed to women within secular and religious arenas were social constructs created by men to ensure that women act within a certain sphere, primarily for men's benefit. Maureen Fitzgerald has noted that although Stanton and Anthony differed in approaches to how women can transcend religious-based subordination in order to acquire public rights and status, they both challenged male prerogative as it related to their own ethnic group. Stanton and Anthony and many other white women in their movement made assumptions that privileged their race, class, and culture. According to Fitzgerald, "analyzing the reasons for the oppression of women in their own group was their greatest strength, and assuming that their condition was equivalent to 'woman's condition'—to the needs and hardships of women of all classes, cultures, races and ethnicities— was their greatest weakness."[20]

As a consequence of Stanton and Anthony centering their own race, class, and culture, what black religious and preaching women were doing at the same time as—and even before—white women is not mentioned in late-nineteenth-century feminist literature or even in contemporary criticism about those white feminists. The result has been the creation of another space where the absence of black women preachers is encoded.

20. Maureen Fitzgerald, "The Religious Is Personal Is Political," foreword to *The Woman's Bible,* by Elizabeth Cady Stanton, xvi.

More studies should be done to explore what is *not* said about how black religious women's works conditioned white women's writings on religion and religious rights. Toni Morrison uses a metaphor that is particularly relevant to white women's using silence to encode an absence of black women's role in religious discourse. Morrison maintains that African American presence informs how whites define themselves, and that this presence "has shaped the choices, language and structure" of 'white' American literature even when they consciously try to deny it." Critics of the literature should engage in the process of searching for the "unspeakable things unspoken." They should search, Morrison states further, "for the ghost in the machine." Black religious women who have such a "great, ornamental, prescribed" absence from nineteenth-century religious discourse should also send us in search for the "holy ghost" in the machine—for ways in which their own spiritual beliefs and insights influenced the writing strategies and religious discourse in the nineteenth century.[21]

Finally, the dialogic nature of prophesying daughters' texts, their ability to touch on so many areas, leads me to emphasize the importance of a cross-disciplinary approach to interpreting these texts in order to get a more complex understanding of them and the culture out of which they were produced. If, as Bakhtin's dialogism suggests, "everything means, is understood, as part of a greater whole—[and] there is a constant interaction between meanings, all of which have the potential of conditioning others," then the boundaries we have set up across academic disciplines need to be destablized as well to fully understand these religious women's texts." I draw, then, from Michel Foucault's model of interdisciplinary discourse and have relied on literary, historical, feminist, liberation theology, biblical studies, and cultural criticism to understand the complexity of these texts. I agree with Gayraud Wilmore's assertion that "an understanding of African American religion and culture cannot be validated without reference to a variety of academic disciplines from both the theological seminaries and the university."[22]

---

21. Toni Morrison, "Unspeakable Things Unspoken: The Afro-American Presence in American Literature," 377.

22. Bakhtin, *Dialogic Imagination,* xiii; Gayraud Wilmore, introduction to *African American Religious Studies: An Interdisciplinary Anthology,* xv.

I begin my study of black women preachers in 1823 with the publication of Jarena Lee's autobiography, and I end it in 1913 with the publication of Frances Joseph Gaudet's autobiography. Covering over a century (Lee's text was published in 1823, but the material in it provides insight on her life dating as far back as the mid-1700s), these texts reveal a wealth of historical insight about prophesying daughters' lives and the culture and society in which they lived. Because I also study Julia Foote's 1879 text and Maria Stewart's 1835 text, we see first of all a development of a history of black women prophesying, with various themes and motifs being employed and altered over the century.[23]

I am not arguing for a transhistorical notion of the act of prophesying. The black religious women discussed here negotiated their political and social situations at three very crucial historical moments in black life in the United States: antebellum, postbellum, and turn of the century. As each historical period brought with it variations or shifts in ideologies of race, class, and gender, the written texts of black religious women show them actively challenging and engaging with these changing ideologies. Collectively, the texts of these prophesying daughters reflect an evolution of their political presence within each of the historical moments in which they were most active in their religious careers.

These women, who believed that they were called by God to act, who accepted this call, and who did all they could to live up to their call, wrote their autobiographies as a direct response to this call. They did so in a social context that necessitated a rhetorically strategic use of aspects of the same Christian belief system into which they were converted and which they embraced. They wrote in a context where many of their readers were Christians yet did not trust the merit of the black self-writer's story. Strict guidelines regarding gender roles restricted women's social and political roles. Prevalent also were ideologies that projected the spiritual and intellectual inferiority of blacks.

What influence would writing as a black, Christian woman in this context have on the choices on what and how to write? How do you prove to a doubtful white Christian reader not only that you do have a soul but also that you have been called by their God to save souls, including theirs? Discussions on how religious views such as prophesying dictated

---

23. This notion is discussed in greater detail in chapter six.

and determined the authorial strategies of religious black women writing in the nineteenth century have been limited. In some cases where the issue of religious belief has been addressed, it has been examined mainly in terms of its historical and sociopolitical ramifications. My hope is that this book will map out a few possible ways of understanding how the act of prophesying in the social context of the nineteenth century is used as a rhetorical literary strategy whose implication is evident even in the canon of nineteenth-century and contemporary black writers.

In chapter three, "Prophetic Change: Jarena Lee's and Julia Foote's Uses of Conversion Rhetoric in the Context of Reader Distrust," I discuss how certain notions such as distrust of the white audience of black women writers, the cult of true womanhood, and ideologies projecting black religious and social inferiority necessitated the politicization of the experience of conversion in order for these women to create space for them to preach. These factors influenced not only how these women experienced conversion but also how they employed it rhetorically in their writing. Such strategies entail embarking on the familiarity of conversion rhetoric in the nineteenth century, discursively inverting this Pauline conversion discourse, strategically placing the conversion account at the beginning of the text to make a statement of existence, and detailing personal conflicts and resolutions with converting.

Chapter four, "Prophetic Journeying: The Trope of Travel in Black Women Preachers' Narratives," explores—from metaphorical, literal, and imperial perspectives—the strategic use of the obligation to do apostolic travel as a means to deconstruct nineteenth-century notions of race, class, and gender. By *apostolic travel* I mean that these women paralleled their travel with that of biblical apostles, who traveled to preach the Gospel of Christ; consequently, these women felt that they too must traverse "all the corners of the earth" to preach. Therefore, they traveled to cities throughout the American North and South. Frances Gaudet even traveled abroad. What this means is that there was a presence of black women preachers on boats, stagecoaches, and trains, and this presence altered the very landscape of the American traveling public in the nineteenth century. That they were traveling also necessitated alterations in restrictive and limiting constructions around race and gender. Using religion as their passport while traveling did not shield them from what Julia Foote called "indignities on the account of color." Jarena Lee noted that as "people of color" they were treated "very indifferently indeed," often resulting in their traveling on the decks of boats or being removed from trains to accommodate protesting whites. But their continued travel despite these "indignities" shows a direct protest against such restrictions. Moreover, as women traveling, these prophesying daughters also complicated notions of woman's cultural space. Travel under religious conviction is analyzed in this chapter as a site of resistance to restrictive boundaries.

Chapter five, "Prophetic Reading: Black Women Preachers and Deconstructive Biblical Interpretation," explores how the idea of prophesying is used to challenge prominent interpretations of the Bible that framed blacks and women in subservient and inferior positions. Such notions were the Pauline idea that women should remain silent in the church and the idea that blacks were the descendants of Ham in the Bible, whose "darker" generations were cursed to be the servants of mankind. Such projections reveal that in the nineteenth century a structure of Bible-based discourse existed that dictated identifications of race, class, and gender. Black religious women strategically counter such hegemonic readings of the Bible by reinterpreting the Bible in ways that foreground blacks and women. Through their use of figuralism (relating to certain groups or figures in the Bible) and what I call *typological "gyn"esis* (referring to female figures in the Bible to establish a beginning or genesis for active women in the Bible), black women preachers transformed the Bible into a text that—like most others—was open to the interpretation of the reader and her interpretive context and community. By revealing prevalent interpretations of the Bible as mere interpretations not mandated by the text itself, black women preachers opened up a space for themselves and their listeners to contest the theology that legitimated their own interpretations without giving up on the Bible itself.

Chapter six, "Prophetic Works: Prophesying Daughters and Social Activism—The Case of Frances Joseph Gaudet," places black religious women at the center of the "race women" movements. This chapter focuses on the various institutions formed by black women preachers (orphanages and schools); their active organizational affiliations (conferences, national women's clubs, and so on); their active participation in social uplift programs (such as prison reform and education); and finally, their experiences with politics of publication as religious women. I focus specifically on Frances Joseph Gaudet, demonstrating how the creation of the Normal School for Boys and Girls (which follows the model set forth by Booker T. Washington), her national and international crusades for prison reform, and her women's club involvements show how black women preachers lifted society in their climb to live up to their obligation to God.

Finally, in chapter 7, "Can I Get A Witness?: The Implications of Prophesying for African American Literary Studies," I discuss the significance of these nineteenth-century religious women's texts to the field of African American literature. I propose that their texts give us insight into a theory of prophesying that aims to offer an alternative way of interpreting literature with strong religious imagery. The formative elements of this concept are drawn from the deconstructive acts that were necessary because these women viewed themselves as prophesying daughters. I delineate the terms under which a text can prophesy, and I conclude with an application of this notion to Harriet Wilson's *Incidents in the Life of a Slave Girl.*

THREE

Prophetic Change

JARENA LEE'S AND JULIA FOOTE'S
USES OF CONVERSION RHETORIC IN
THE CONTEXT OF READER DISTRUST

O ne cannot read the narratives of prophesying daughters without noticing the lengths to which they go to describe their conversion experiences. Within the first ten to twenty pages of their narratives, Jarena Lee and Julia Foote, for example, detail their encounters with bright and blinding lights, loud and demanding voices, clear and sometimes frightening visions, and stultifying and incapacitating physical and emotional changes. Julia Foote even couches the title of her narrative in conversion rhetoric, suggesting that as a *Brand Plucked from the Fire,* she has gone through some purifying, trying experience out of which something or someone new has emerged. In addition to detailing their own conversion experiences, they also discuss other people's conversions that came about as a result of their preaching. They state how converts wailed and shouted, fell to floors, and soaked themselves in tears as they converted over to God.

That readers were aware that they went through a conversion experience and had the power to convert others was obviously important to these prophesying daughters. Some scholars have begun to theorize about why, primarily noting reasons of self-empowerment. William Andrews, for example, says that for prophesying daughters, conversion spurred "a very real sense of freedom for a prior 'self' and a growing awareness of unrealized, unexploited powers within." Andrews states further that "after conversion the self is transformed into a 'new creation' free from the bondage of sin and fit for service as an instrument of the divine will." Frances Smith Foster notes that after her conversion experience, Jarena Lee "possessed a power to effect change." Kimberly Connors sees conversion as "an imaginative act of transforming the self through the creation of a new image of self and a new image of God." Finally, Jean Humez recognizes conversion as "clearly a valuable resource in their struggles for autonomy in their personal lives, as well as in their lives as itinerant preachers."[1]

In this chapter, I add to the discussion about the empowerment that the conversion experience gave prophesying daughters and explore their use of conversion as a rhetorical device to break down and challenge nineteenth-century ideologies around race and gender. In keeping with my view of prophesying as a deconstructive endeavor, I analyze this use of conversion within the context of white reader distrust of black writers in the nineteenth century. I contend that knowing that their readers did not trust them as writers meant that talking about conversion served a dual purpose for these prophesying daughters: 1) It had to be used to convert doubtful readers over to accepting them as legitimate Christians called to preach or do God's work, and 2) it had to be inverted (flipping the script again), in order to interrogate limitations that constructs around gender imposed on them but also to defeat these restrictions.

The prophesying daughters employed this rhetorical strategy primarily in their appropriation of the typological account of conversion detailed by Paul (Saul of Tarsus) in the Bible, which is commonly referred to as the first detailed conversion. This account was also quite familiar to most nineteenth-century readers. Prophesying daughters detailed their conversions to show that their experiences directly replicated Paul's in an attempt to prove that their conversions were legitimate. However, after doing so, they experienced a dilemma: Even though they used Paul's conversion as an iconic base from which to prove their legitimate Christian being, they were also in a position where they had to invert certain Pauline notions being used in the nineteenth century to justify their inferior social status as women. I explore their engaging in what I call a discursive inversion of such Pauline discourse.

1. Andrews, *Sisters of the Spirit,* 13; ibid.; Foster, *Written by Herself,* 74; Kimberly Rae Connor, *Conversions and Visions in the Writings of African-American Women,* 15; Jean Humez, " 'My Spirit Eye': Some Functions of Spiritual and Visionary Experiences in the Lives of Five Black Women Preachers, 1810–1880," 130.

My discussion of these black women preachers' strategic use of conversion discourse is conceptually rooted in the critical discussions of the conversion experience that have posited that societal guidelines influence the ways in which converts report their experience. James Beckford, for example—in his study on accounts of conversion by Jehovah's Witnesses—asserts that their "conversion accounts are typically constructed according to a set of guidelines which reflects the Watchtower Movement's changing organizational rationale."[2] Beckford maintains that various ideologies within the movement dictated rules for speaking about conversion. I maintain that various ideologies of distrust dictated how prophesying daughters chose to write about their conversion. Before discussing this use of conversion, it is important first to discuss the notion of reader distrust and its impact on the writing strategies of black women autobiographers in the nineteenth century.

The autobiography for African American women in the nineteenth century was not only an act of telling the stories of their lives but also an act of proving and verifying their lives in an effort to inscribe themselves into literary history. One factor that made it necessary to verify themselves in their writing was the relationship that black women writers had with a predominantly white readership, a relationship predicated on preconceived notions about the inferiority of blacks. Informed by a history of slavery, this relationship was characterized by skepticism, distrust, and sometimes disdain for the black self-writer. "Knowing that they could not assume an equal relationship with the average White American reader," many black women autobiographers in the nineteenth century "set about writing their life stories that would somehow prove that they qualified as the moral, spiritual, or intellectual peers of whites."[3]

Despite this distrust of their abilities, black women continued to tell their stories. "Testimonials" of writers such as Harriet Jacobs (1861), Elizabeth Keckley (1868), Mary Prince (1831), Nancy Prince (1853), and several others reveal the complex, heterogeneous make-up of African American female subjectivity in the nineteenth-century context. Black women were either slaves, ex-slaves, free, educated, or uneducated. Their narratives proved to many doubtful readers not only that they existed

---

2. James Beckford, "Accounting for Conversion," 1.
3. Andrews, *To Tell a Free Story,* 2.

but also that their existence was characterized by social and moral consciousness and an awareness of themselves in a social context that rendered them subjectless. Joanne Braxton's *Black Women Writing Autobiography* reveals the many ways that African American women, in spite of this distrust, used autobiography as a form of self-construction and as a medium for revealing their thoughts, responses, and reactions to nineteenth-century society.

To proclaim, as prophesying daughters did, that the image in which they saw and constructed themselves was created and validated by the Christian God inspired even more doubt for many readers. Not only were they, as African Americans, already challenging common perceptions by claiming to have the intellectual capacity to write, but also, as women, they were crossing gender boundaries that had clearly marked distinctions. Women in the nineteenth century simply were not expected to be preachers. African American women certainly were not.

Nowhere is this point better illustrated than in a letter prefacing Julia Foote's autobiography. T. K. Doty, editor of the *Christian Harvester* newspaper, notes that Foote was "guilty of three great crimes" (*Brand,* 5). Doty goes on to state that the first crime that Foote was guilty of is "that of Color. For, though not now the slaves of individual men, our brethren continue to be under the bondage of society" (*Brand,* 5). "In the next place," Doty continues, "we see the crime of Womanhood. As though any one, with heart and lips of love, may not speak further the praises of Him who hath called us out of darkness into light" (*Brand,* 5). The last crime, Doty notes, is that "our sister, as stated, is an evangelist" (*Brand,* 5). Like much of African American literature in the nineteenth century, Doty's introduction serves as a letter of authentication. Such a document anticipates reader doubt and skepticism about blacks' intellectual abilities, and it serves as an attempt to offset this distrust by having a prominent member of the community put his (or sometimes her) name and reputation on the line by testifying to the veracity of the black writer's story.

One of the most popular instances of this use of authenticating documents can be seen in the letter prefacing Phillis Wheatley's *Poems of Various Subjects.* Here, Thomas Hutchinson, governor of Massachusetts; John Hancock, signer of the Declaration of Independence; Reverend Charles Chauncey, pastor of the Tenth Congregational Church; and fifteen other prominent citizens of Boston signed their name to a letter, stating that they

> do assure the World, that the Poems specified in the following Pages, were (as we verily believe) written by Phillis, a young Negro Girl, who was but a few years since, brought an uncultivated Barbarian from *Africa,* and has ever since been, and now is, under the Disadvantage of serving as a Slave in a Family in this town. She has been examined by some of the best Judges, and is thought qualified to write them.[4]

Although slavery had ended when Foote was writing her narrative, blacks were still, as Doty states, "under the bondage of society." The Black Codes and Jim Crow laws were relegating blacks to the slums, to balconies of churches, and to decks of boats. Foote herself, in a chapter she entitles "Indignities on Account of Color," writes candidly about an incident where a passenger on board a boat refused to enter where she was by shouting that "that nigger has no business here. My family is on board the boat to Utica, and shall not come where a nigger is" (*Brand,* 91).

Doty's couching his preface to Foote's autobiography within a discourse of criminality—in phrases that suggest there is something wrong with or "criminal" about being black, woman, and preacher—sheds insight into the context of reader distrust confronting prophesying daughters in the nineteenth century. This letter indicates that like many African American women autobiographers in the nineteenth century, prophesying daughters wrote under special conditions and constraints. They labored to find language and discourse that would articulate the validity of the God-inspired image in which they defined and viewed themselves, an image that was created during their conversion experience.

Research by Barbara Epstein indicates that black religious women had models available to them on how to write about their conversion experiences and their new images. In her discussion of how men and women experienced conversion in the nineteenth century, Epstein notes how the widespread conversions that began to take place during the revivalist period (Second Great Awakening) resulted in the appearance of varied accounts of conversions in evangelical journals, newspapers,

---

4. Julian Mason Jr., ed., *The Poems of Phillis Wheatley,* 48.

and pamphlets.[5] In fact, prophesying daughters even detailed their own participation in revival meetings, and—as was typical in many of the journals of their day—they also detailed the number of people who were converted, the outpourings of emotions that occurred during their conversions, and the intensity of the conversions. Jarena Lee, for example, details the following conversions that happened under her auspices within the context of distrust. She describes her participation in a service at a meetinghouse, "whose preacher was skeptical of [her] abilities as a preacher" (*Experience*, 24). According to Lee, "He said he did not believe that ever a soul was converted under the preaching of a woman—but while I was laboring in his place, conviction seized a woman, who fell to the floor crying for mercy" (*Experience*, 24). She describes conversions that occurred at another revival meeting she preached: "We had pentecostal showers—sinners were pricked to the heart, and cried mightily to God for succor from impending judgement, and I verily believe the Lord was well pleased at our weak endeavors to serve him in the tented grove" (*Experience*, 28).

These types of conversion accounts, according to Epstein, contain encoded guidelines of acceptable behavior during conversion based on gender. Men, according to Epstein, were "reluctant converts" because of nineteenth-century emphasis on emotional constraint for men. Women, on the other hand, because of emphasis on emotionalism, "were much more emotional and experienced God more intensely." They detailed these feelings in their accounts. Epstein states further that any confusion, anxiety, or rebellious feelings women may have felt because of these intense feelings were to be replaced with "joyful submission."[6]

Epstein focuses primarily on what she calls the "typical" nineteenth-century woman convert. As "typical," these white middle-class women—even when they felt opposition from resisting husbands or males—still were privileged in that they were at least granted the spiritual right to conversion because of their race, even if it was within certain guidelines.[7] In many instances, black women who converted within a social context

5. Barbara Epstein, *The Politics of Domesticity: Women, Evangelism, and Temperance in Nineteenth-Century America*, 55.

6. Ibid., 55, 58.

7. Epstein also notes in this essay that many women were confronted with resistance from husbands, who thought that their wives were crossing acceptable boundaries by attending these public revival meetings. Also, after converting, many

of distrust had limitations on how they were to experience conversion. Blacks were perceived by many whites as possessing extreme, almost animalistic emotionalism that would have no sufficient avenue for expression in the controlled, very restricted phraseology required to recount "typical" conversion experiences. This, coupled with assertions that blacks did not even have souls to convert, complicated even further their own negotiations with how to record their conversion experiences.

Yet they knew that they were converted and called, and that they were therefore obligated to live up to God's command. That they wrote about their conversion dictates a consideration of the cultural effect of ideologies of distrust of black women's religious identity on their writing about conversion. It is important to situate their narratives within general expectations about what conversion indicated or how it was to be discussed if one is to comprehend and analyze the ways in which prophesying daughters used their writing to subvert religious ideological codes. In writing their conversions, prophesying daughters had to convert the skeptics they confronted into accepting the validity of their God-called subjectivity. In this sense, conversion became a dilemma and an opportunity for prophesying daughters.

How did they seize upon this opportunity? By recognizing that in order to break down barriers of distrust, they had to use models familiar to their readers. What better narrative to employ for their purposes than that of Paul (Saul of Tarsus)? John Lofland and Norman Skonovd have noted that Paul's conversion "has in a sense functioned as the ideal of what conversion should be in the Western world."[8] Paul's conversion from being the antithesis of Christian views into a representative synthesis of those views testified to the power of divine intervention in using the once-despised as an advocate. The Pauline conversion becomes a metaphor for authentic Christian being that prophesying daughters used and with which they aligned themselves. They did so strategically, by taking their readers through their own process of conversion, which replicated Paul's. In order to illustrate how they employed this tactic, it is important to first outline the phases of Paul's conversion.

---

women started challenging their husbands' right to question their public excursions for God, feeling more obligated to please God than their husbands.

8. Lofland and Skonovd, "Conversion Motifs," 376.

As detailed in the book of Acts, Paul went through an initial phase of ignorance and corruption characterized by spiritual uncertainty. In this phase, Paul was executing and imprisoning anyone who professed to be a Christian. He did so by making "havoc of the church, entering every house, and dragging off men and women, committing them to prison" (Acts 8:3).[9] From a societal perspective, Paul had no location in relation to the Christian God or the Scriptures except in the negative capacity of keeping as many people as possible away from converting or having a relationship with God. His change, however, was signaled by intense visions, lights, and voices. While en route to Damascus to conduct more persecutions, Paul's conversion was initiated by a strong voice and a blinding light: "Suddenly a light shone around him from heaven. Then he fell to the ground and heard a voice" (Acts 9:3,4). He also experienced changes to his body: "And he was three days without sight, and neither ate nor drank" (Acts 9:9). Paul's conversion was further accompanied by an intermediary, Ananias, who had received instruction from God in a dream to tell Paul how to receive his calling. Ananias instructed Paul to "arise and go into the city and you will be told what you must do," and he was told to preach (Acts 9:6).

The biblical account of Paul's conversion does not give a direct indication of his hesitancy to preach. However, one can speculate that he knew that preaching would be difficult for him. When he first hears the voice, he is "trembling and astonished," first, for fear of God; second, for fear of what lay ahead. As a convert into a religious culture that he had denounced, he had to have been concerned about how he would be perceived. People were understandably skeptical about his sincerity and his calling, asking questions such as, "is this not he who destroyed those who called on his name in Jerusalem" (Acts 9:16). Even other disciples were skeptical of him: "and when Paul had come to Jerusalem, he tried to join the disciples; but they were all afraid of him, and did not believe that he was a disciple" (Acts 9:26). Aside from being doubted by Christians, Paul also had to contend with the ridicule and disdain he would receive from those who hired him in the beginning to kill the Christians. So surely Paul was apprehensive about taking on such a challenge. He made the transition, however, and accepted his call, going on "to speak

9. Acts 8:3. All biblical quotations are taken from the *Oxford Study Bible* and are hereafter cited parenthetically by chapter and verse.

boldly in the name of the Lord" (Acts 2:29). He traveled extensively to convert people to Christianity. He wrote the Epistles in order to change the social order and to convert others to God.

Jarena Lee and Julia Foote detail their conversion experiences in a way that replicates Paul's directly. Just as Paul's preconversion life was characterized by a state of spiritual vacancy, so are their preconversion lives presented. This is evidenced in the emphasis on episodes of severe depression or suicidal tendencies prior to being converted. Lee, for example, speaks of several times when she was "tempted to destroy herself" (*Experience*, 4). Foote states as well that she "wished over and over again to be hanged" (*Brand*, 25).

As with most autobiography—but particularly that which describes some kind of religious change brought about by conversion—one must consider the issue of retro-interpretation, or looking at and explaining one's life in retrospect. The present from which Lee and Foote recounted their past lives was shaped and informed by an experience that changed their view of the world and themselves. Certain events, when being recounted, are magnified or deemphasized from this perspective. In engaging in this process that social theorists call "biographical reconstruction," Lee and Foote interpret the "sinful nature" that distinguishes their preconverted lives from their postconverted lives as being the consequence of God's absence and Satan's presence in their lives. Whereas Paul's lack of knowledge and awareness of God's goodness can be seen in his persecuting, hurting, and killing other people, Lee's and Foote's ignorance of God can be seen in their attempts to hurt or kill themselves. For example, Lee attributes her suicidal tendencies to her lack of knowledge of God, which created in her a sense of vulnerability to Satan: "[A] condition struck me to the heart, and made me feel in some measure the weight of my sin, and sinful nature. But not knowing how to run immediately to the Lord for help, I was driven by Satan, in the course of a few days, and tempted to destroy myself" (*Experience,* 4). Likewise, Foote interprets her suicidal tendencies as being the result of divine ignorance, asserting that "in the darkness and silence, Satan came to me and told me to go to the barn and hang myself" (*Brand,* 25). The morning after this alleged demand from Satan, Foote "was fully determined to do so," but she was distracted by a young boy who was in the barn (*Brand,* 25). Because of this distraction, Foote felt that "thus I was saved from a dreadful sin" (*Brand,* 25). Lee and Foote do not align themselves with Paul's prespiritual stage to comply with or to validate nineteenth-century notions of black spiritual incapability or inferiority. Rather, they use this as a strategy to suggest that because society portrays blacks as incapable of spiritual life and offers them no means of expressing spiritual experiences when they do have religious experiences and spiritual inclinations, there may seem to some no alternative other than suicide.

To signal their initiation into the conversion process, Lee and Foote use the same rhetoric of lights, visions, and voices that was used to describe the initiation of Paul's conversion. Lee describes her vision as appearing suddenly and revealing to her the dreadful place to which she is headed if she continues the life in which she "rejoiced in the vanities of life" (*Experience*, 5). In this vision, she explains that "an awful gulf of hell seemed to be open beneath me, covered only, as it were, by a spider's web, on which I stood. I seemed to hear the howling of the damned, to see the smoke of the bottomless pit, and hear the rattling of those chains, which hold the impenitent under clouds of darkness to the judgment of the great day" (*Experience*, 6). Paul experienced physical changes, as evidenced by his being temporarily blinded. Lee describes experiencing a physical change as well: "My strength had left me, I had become feverish and sickly through the violence of my feeling" (*Experience*, 6).

Foote, who also describes her preconversion life as being characterized by pursuing "the pomps and vanities of this life," details experiencing a blinding light and hearing a voice as well. She says that "something within me kept saying 'Such a sinner as you can never sing that new song'" (*Brand*, 32). This "something," she understands, is the voice of God, and the "new song" is that sung by one who is knowledgeable of God. Once she asks God to save her from sin, the voice "ceased at once" (*Brand*, 33). After the voice leaves, "a ray of light flashed across [her] eyes . . . , the light grew lighter," and, according to Foote, "such joy and peace filled my heart when I felt I was redeemed" (*Brand*, 33).

The intermediary in Paul's conversion—or the conveyor of the message of God—is Ananias. For Lee and Foote, this intermediary is a preacher, and the message of God is transmitted through the preacher's voice during a sermon. Lee's calling was accompanied by Richard Allen, founder of the African Methodist Episcopal Church. She recounts that "during the labors of this man that afternoon . . . I embraced the opportunity" to be converted (*Experience*, 5). She states further that shortly after hearing his sermon, "my soul was gloriously converted to God, under preaching, at the very outbreak of the sermon" (*Experience*, 5).

Foote recalls that "As the minister dwelt with great force and power on the first clause of the text, I beheld my lost condition as I never had done before. . . . I fell to the floor, unconscious and was carried home. . . . *Every converted man and women can imagine what my feelings were*" (*Brand*, 32; my emphasis). At this point, Foote finds it necessary to interject dialogue with any reader who may have experienced conversion. She is doing this so that she can note that any reader who has gone through this Pauline conversion can at least relate to her experience. It is important that she talks to the reader at this point. Any white reader who can admit that she or he has experienced such blinding lights, such feelings of vulnerability and weakness while converting, will have to admit or acknowledge that Foote is indeed telling the truth. If this is the case, the reader is also acknowledging the legitimacy of Foote's feelings, which in turn means recognizing her humanity. If every white man or woman who has converted can "imagine" Foote experiencing what they too have gone through, then they must "imagine" her as a spiritual equal.

In accounts that mirror that of Paul's conversion, where he is instructed by God to go preach, both Lee and Foote detail receiving the same instructions. Lee writes that she was instructed to "Go preach the gospel" (*Experience*, 10). "Preach the Gospel without the delay" are the instructions that Foote details she received. However, just as Paul must have been apprehensive about accepting his call to preach because of the skepticism of the disciples and other Christians, Lee and Foote also inscribe their apprehension. Foote addresses her apprehension directly to God: "When called of God . . . I said 'No Lord, not me.' . . . I thought that it could not be that I was called to preach—, so weak and ignorant" (*Brand*, 65). Lee recalls that "my courage began to fail me. So terrible did that cross appear. It seemed that I should not be able to bear it" (*Experience*, 11).

People were skeptical of Paul because he was a persecutor and murderer of Christians. For Lee and Foote, gender differentiations that were very prevalent in the nineteenth century informed their doubt and apprehension. They knew that as women trying to preach in a male-dominated field, they would be met with skepticism and opposition. It is this anticipated doubt that made Lee exclaim that "No one will believe me," for she knew that it was "unseemly . . . now-a-days for a woman to preach" (*Experience,* 11). Foote admits that present constructs about women's prescribed roles in the church informed her own self-doubt about accepting her call: "I had always been opposed to the preaching of women, and had spoken against it. . . . This rose before me like a mountain, and when I thought of the difficulties they had to encounter from both professors and non-professors, I shrank back and cried, 'Lord, I can not go!'" (*Brand,* 67). Accepting this responsibility would mean breaking away from the traditional role that women played in the church. This was understandably frightening.

Paul eventually accepted his calling and did whatever possible to preach God's words. He went on "to speak boldly in the name of the Lord" (Acts 2:29), traveling all over his country to convert people to Christianity. He wrote the Epistles as an effort to change the social order. Lee and Foote finally attained the confidence in their ability to preach. Upon accepting her calling, Foote acknowledges that "I can no longer be shaken by what . . . anyone else may think or say" (*Brand,* 72). Of her acceptance, Lee states that "Since that time . . . I have not doubted the power and goodness of God to keep me from falling, through the sanctification of the spirit and the belief of the truth" (*Experience,* 13).

Using Paul's conversion account to situate themselves ontologically within the Christian context was indeed a very strategic move, one that also positioned prophesying daughters to critique the social guidelines that excluded them. Just as Paul was able to transcend traditional expectations of discipleship, so could they transcend traditional gender roles in the nineteenth century. They felt that just as Paul was able after his conversion, as Lee stated, "to preach the same gospel which he had neglected and despised," their conversion, which replicated his, enabled them to transcend their preconverted status as "neglected" and "despised" women who were also black. However, just as Paul's conversion proved liberating for them in one sense, other language written by Paul created a major dilemma for them. In the nineteenth century, Pauline discourse inscribed in his Epistles was also being used to justify gender constructs that defined male behavior or roles as public and assertive and women's roles as private and submissive. Several passages were being used to support this projection of female behavior. One of the most popular scriptures used came from Paul's letter to the Corinthians in 1 Corinthians 14:34–35: "Let your women keep silent in the churches, for they are not permitted to speak, but they are to be submissive, as the law also says. And if they want to learn something, let them ask their own husbands at home." Noting that the Bible mandated that women "keep silent in the churches" supported views that women preaching went against biblical law. How could they be silent and preach? The assertion that they "are to be submissive" maintains the established male title of the head of the church and household and reemphasizes the notion of woman's deference to him. Moreover, the directive that women "ask their husbands at home" anything they wanted to know further stresses that women should remain in the private space of the home and stay away from the masculine space represented in arenas such as politics and the pulpit.[10]

For prophesying daughters, this created tension. Yes, they were women and black, but they had gone through a legitimate conversion and had resolved, like Paul, to live up to God's commands. In fact, Jarena Lee, when she fully accepted her call to preach, used Pauline discourse to describe the seriousness of her conviction: "Now I could adopt the very language of St. Paul, and say, that nothing could have separated me from the love of God, which is in Christ Jesus" (*Experiencnce*, 13). Nineteenth-century use of Paul's words to keep them out of the pulpit, then, put them in a predicament where they had to critique the oppressive use of Paul's very words without having to give up on them.[11] They were able to invert the use of this discourse by offering alternative views. When dominant society used the Pauline scripture that women are to be submissive and "silent" in church and society, Julia Foote offered another perspective. Foote maintains that women should not be "kept in bondage by those who say, 'we suffer not a woman to teach,' thus quoting Paul's words but not rightly applying them" (*Brand*, 113). She critiques this scripture-based gender restriction by calling attention to a very important point about historical contextualization. She recognizes that one should not divorce the meaning of an idea or act from

10. This public/private dichotomy that in many ways shaped and defined social spheres has been the subject of analysis by many feminists, who note how this ideology maintained women's submissive roles. For thorough consideration of this idea, see Mary Douglas, *Purity and Danger: An Analysis of Concepts of Pollution and Taboo*. See also Mary Ryan, *Cradle of the Middle Class: The Family in Oneida County, New York, 1790–1865*; and Epstein, *Politics of Domesticity*.

11. For another assessment of how other biblical arguments were used to maintain women's subservient roles, see Barbara Brown Zikmund, "Biblical Arguments and Women's Place in the Church."

its original historical or sociological context. Nineteenth-century interpreters, to her, are therefore "not rightly using [the Scriptures]." Prescribed guidelines for female roles and behavior in Paul's times were not necessarily applicable to "modern" times. Women were in very different positions in the nineteenth century than they were in Paul's day, and to expect them to live according to expectations of another historical time period seemed unrealistic to many prophesying daughters. Foote strongly suggests that it is not that the Bible prescribed silence for women, but rather that nineteenth-century society adopted this interpretation in an effort to keep women in "bondage." It becomes necessary and important to dismiss or ignore these constructs or opinions. Recognizing such negative readings of women's positions as man's own view, man's own opinion, Foote asserts that "Man's opinion weighed nothing to me" (*Brand*, 78).

Foote also shows flaws in nineteenth-century society's use of Pauline scriptures by interpreting women's participation in Paul's ministry as active instead of submissive. She states rather sarcastically that "when Paul said 'Help those who labor with me in the Gospel,' he certainly meant that they did more than just pour out tea" (*Brand*, 79). This phrase illustrates Foote's rejection of being framed in a traditional domestic role. Not only do these black women preachers see themselves as being like the active women in Paul's ministry, but they also see themselves as being like Paul.

One final way that prophesying daughters used conversion discourse within the context of reader distrust can be seen in the strategic positioning of the account of the experience itself. In each of the texts, the conversion account appears in the first few pages of their narratives. Strategically, this is done in order to establish up front their legitimacy as Christian subjects. Placing this conversion experience at the beginning of the narratives as a way to authenticate their existence continues an African American literary tradition seen particularly in the narratives of slaves. Letters of authentication that prefaced the texts of many slave narratives—along with the existential claim that "I was born" that usually begins the actual narrative—are characteristic of this genre.

Many narratives begin with letters from prominent members of the community that attest to the veracity of the person and his or her story that is to follow. Frederick Douglass's narrative, for example, has a letter from famed abolitionist William Lloyd Garrison that vouches that

Douglass's narrative is "entirely his own production; and considering how long and dark was the career he had to run as a slave,—how few have been his opportunities to improve his mind since he broke his iron fetters,—it is, in my judgment, highly credible to his head and heart." Lydia Maria Child, the white woman editor of Harriet Jacobs's autobiography, assures readers that "the author of the following autobiography is personally known to me, and her conversation and manners inspire me with confidence." She states further that "those who know her will not be disposed to doubt her veracity."[12] Providing such letters of attestation from prominent and respected members of the white community was done as an editorial attempt to convince a reading audience to force themselves outside of their preconceived notions about the unintelligibility of blacks and to trust that the former slave actually did write his or her story.

Another common feature of the slave narratives was the consistency with which the vast majority of them began with the claim "I was born." By beginning their narratives with the subjective "I," these black writers not only provide a powerful statement and notification of their being, but they also force the reader to acknowledge their existence and subjectivity from the onset. James Olney best summarizes the significance of the letters of authentication and the "I was born" statement:

> [T]he argument of the slave narratives is that the events narrated are factual and truthful and that they all really happened to the narrator, but this is a second stage argument: prior to the claim of truthfulness is the simple, existential claim: "I exist." Photographs, portraits, signatures, authenticating letters all make the same claim: "This man exists." Only then can the narrative begin. And how do most of them actually begin? They begin with the existential claim repeated.[13]

Olney analyzes the dialectic involved in the relationship between the slave narrator and the existing marginalizing and self-negating ideologies that preclude the act of writing for blacks. Reader doubt—informed

12. Frederick Douglass, *Narrative of the Life of Frederick Douglass, An American Slave, Written by Himself,* 248; Harriet Jacobs, *Incidents in the Life of a Slave Girl,* 337.
13. James Olney, " 'I Was Born': Slave Narratives, Their Status as Autobiography and as Literature," 149.

primarily by racial prejudices—impacts the narrative strategies of the black writer, necessitating the use of actualizing devices such as the photographs and letters Olney mentions.

Lee and Foote continue this tradition in that they provide letters of authentication, and the "I was born" claim appears almost immediately in their texts. However, their position as prophesying daughters compels them to amend the use of the existential claim and authenticating letters and documents Olney establishes. Although they do provide letters from prominent community members, they follow them with an authorial statement that acknowledges society's tendency to marginalize them on the basis of race and gender. Then they make the existential claim "I was born." However, because they are declaring themselves to be Christians, they must finally make the existential claim "I was reborn" into Christian being. This claim is made, I argue, in their strategic positioning of the conversion experience.

For example, Jarena Lee, before making use of her conversion experience, prefaces her existential claim with a quote from Joel 2:28, which states that "and it shall come to pass . . . that I shall pour out my spirit upon all flesh; and your sons and your daughters will prophesy." This statement, placed at the beginning of the narrative, anticipates reader enmity. It is telling the reader before he or she even reads the text that it has been divinely mandated that she as a woman has the right to prophesy. Interestingly, too, is her conscious choice not to mention race in this prefatory statement. It is a subversive way of saying that race has not been divinely singled out either, and it therefore should not be determinative of her legitimacy as a preacher. She then makes her statement "I was born February 11, 1783, at Cape May, State of New Jersey" in this nongendered and nonracialized divine space (*Experience,* 3).

Likewise, Foote—who titles her first chapter after the quote in her title page—continues this motif. Quoting Zechariah 3:2, "Is not this a brand plucked out of the fire?", Foote is asserting her subjectivity. The fire is synonymous with the hardships and trials she as a black women writer in the nineteenth century endures when confronted with the complications entailed in being "estranged from the white reader by a slave past."[14] By identifying herself as a brand, Foote portrays herself as a legitimate,

---

14. William Andrews, "The Novelization of Voice in Early African American Narratives," 23.

self-acknowledged subject that has been "plucked" from the margin and placed in the center to complicate and interrogate it. She then makes her existential claim that "I was born in 1823, in Schenectady, N.Y." in the center of a divinely mandated space (*Brand*, 9).

The traditional narrative techniques of providing letters of authentication, acknowledging and dismissing reader enmity, and making their existential claim are used in the prophesying daughters' discussion of the conversion experience to make the same kind of ontological claim to doubtful readers. Like the prominent community members who wrote letters as authorities for the slave narrators, God—in his participation in their conversion experience—becomes the writer of their letter of authentication as legitimate Christian subjects. It is the God-induced conversion that gives them the authority as well to make the secondary existential claim that "I was born again." Placing the conversion experience at or near the beginning of the texts so that they can state that they were born again dispels the idea that blacks had no souls and were incapable of prophesying. It also dispels the notion that women could not prophesy, by suggesting that God—in selecting and interfacing with them through conversion—apparently did not have a gender bias. Social constructs, not divine ones, limit women.

Jarena Lee's and Julia Foote's records of their conversion processes represent how crucial the experience was to prophesying daughters. It gave them confidence in their call. It empowered them to see themselves as legitimate Christian beings. Even though they maintained this view of themselves, many whites did not, so conversion also became a space for inversion of such limited, exclusionary perceptions.

FOUR

Prophetic Journeying

THE TROPE OF TRAVEL IN BLACK WOMEN PREACHERS' NARRATIVES

I n an 1826 travel sketch describing a trip on a steamboat across the Canadian lakes, Nathaniel Hawthorne wrote that as a passenger, one is afforded "opportunities for a varied observation of society." Hawthorne observed from what he described as a "spacious" ship, that "there were three different orders of passengers: an aristocracy, in the grand cabin and ladies saloon; a commonality in the forward cabin; and lastly, a male and female multitude on the forward deck."[1] Hawthorne's "varied observation" indicates that a large and diverse group of people was traveling in nineteenth-century America. The sketch indicates as well that clear class and gender categories separated travelers and went unquestioned, even by Hawthorne. Writing as a passenger "in the grand cabin," Hawthorne describes the condition of travel and his fellow travelers from a position of privilege, glossing over passengers of the other sections as the "commonality" and "multitudes." His observation, "varied" as it seems, nonetheless ignores consideration of the individuals who were on the decks, their purposes for travel, and their destinations. Yet these "multitudes" can tell us even more about American society from their own "varied observations."

Among those traveling on the decks of such steamboats were prophesying daughters such as Jarena Lee and Julia Foote. Their accounts of their excursions contrast greatly with Hawthorne's. Describing her voyage on a similar steamboat ride to Ontario in the early 1800s, Jarena

1. Alfred Weber, Beth L. Lueck, and Dennis Berthold, eds., *Hawthorne's American Travel Sketches,* 49.

Lee notes that the trip was "the most uncomfortable passage I have ever experienced, although the boat was commodious, yet they treated the people of color very indifferently indeed, as regards to their accommodations" (*Experience*, 72). Although, as Mary Schriber indicates, "all travelers tolerated inconveniences and many of them withstood considerable discomfort," Foote's "most uncomfortable" experience was exacerbated by the inferior amenities to which she was limited because of her race.[2] Schriber notes how traveling in America and abroad created extreme difficulties for all travelers. While accounts of many nineteenth-century white middle-class travelers do indicate that they did indeed experience seasickness, fatigue, and other discomforts, I would argue that these conditions were far worse for black travelers, who shared space with mail and other cargo and who had to ride on the decks of steamships, enduring rain and other extreme weather conditions.

We see further evidence of these substandard travel conditions in Julia Foote's description of one of her steamboat rides, an experience likewise different from Hawthorne's. She describes how she caught a severe cold from the damp air on the deck of a steamboat because, as she states, "prejudice [was] not permitting one of my color to enter the cabin, except in the capacity of a servant" (*Brand*, 96). In detailing her travel account, Foote calls into question the differing racial ideologies that led to the actual cultural and social isolation and exclusion that black travelers encountered. Foote was correct that the only way they were granted access to the grand cabin of Hawthorne's sketch was in the socially acceptable role of a servant.

Why then, considering such obvious hardships and severe maltreatment, did Lee, Foote, and other black religious women continue to travel as far west as Kansas, as far north as Canada, and as far south as Louisiana? Why did these particular black religious women insist on enduring the bad conditions on the decks of boats and in the mail section of stagecoaches or trains, sometimes even traveling by foot? Why did they feel it necessary to chronicle their travel experiences in their narratives? What factors influenced why and how they chose to write about their travel? At the core of the answer to these questions is a notion I am calling the *prophetic journey*.

2. Mary Suzanne Schriber, ed., *Writing Home: American Women Abroad, 1830–1920*, 18.

Thousands of Americans were traveling in the nineteenth century, and for various reasons: for expansion and growth, for leisure, vacation, and even escape. What distinguishes the travel of these particular women is the element of religious conviction, the idea that they took seriously God's command of them to "go ye therefore and teach all nations." Obviously these nineteenth-century black religious women were not unique in their feeling a moral obligation to convert and save souls. Numerous scholarly texts have been written about the scores of missionaries traveling domestically and abroad to fulfill a moral obligation and the large religious movements resulting in mass conversions. What makes these women's journeys prophetic are their conditions as blacks and women traveling for God against the backdrop of contradictory, exclusive, and restrictive ideologies. Their metaphorical and literal movement for God positioned them such that they had to deconstruct, challenge, and redefine race, class, and gender ideologies. Writing about their travels in their narratives was one way to leave evidence of their struggle to adhere to this command, and in chronicling their journeys for God these black religious women developed an alternative narrative of prophetic journeying.

Because prophetic journeying involves the act of interrogation and deconstruction, it is in some ways similar to Marilyn Wesley's concept of the "secret journey" of white women travelers in the nineteenth century. According to Wesley, the travels of these white women can be seen as "secret" because of the historical occlusion of their travel stories in the traditional nineteenth-century white male travel texts, which tended to depict the woman traveler as acquiescent. In reading the actual accounts of these "secret" texts, Wesley observes that they provide "radical challenges to dominant social values organized by gender and conveyed by culture." By challenging these dominant structures, the secret journey is "always a figure of deconstruction."[3]

The travel accounts of black women preachers also are secret in the sense in which Wesley uses the term. Hawthorne's glossing over of the multitudes on the deck of the ship he was on provides a strong example of how the stories from the decks become suppressed, are made "secret" or silent in male narratives of privilege. Also, the accounts of travels

---

3. Marilyn Wesley, *Secret Journeys: The Trope of Women's Travel in American Literature,* xiii.

by black male travelers and itinerant preachers often occluded women's stories. For example, in his autobiography, Richard Allen—the founder of the African Methodist Episcopal Church with which Jarena Lee was affiliated—makes references to women during his travels but provides very little insight about them and their views while traveling. Reverend Daniel Payne—another bishop and historian of the A.M.E. church—in his recordings of his years of missionary work, makes mention of his wife but offers very little detail about how she may have responded to their experiences. Even a male slave narrator such as Frederick Douglass leaves out details of the assistance women provided him while he participated in diverted travel.[4] Lee's and Foote's accounts of their own experiences on the decks of those boats and their critique of the racist system responsible for their marginalization do indeed provide "radical challenges to dominant social values."

Applying Wesley's idea of the secret journey to black women preachers becomes complicated, though, when we factor in their religious conviction and the role that it played in their perception of themselves as prophesying daughters. As prophesying daughters, they were traveling under the direction of God, a higher authority that, to them, superseded all manmade, earthly constructs. Traveling under His direction authorized them to put forth challenges not only to the same class and gender categories being challenged in the secret journeys of white women's texts but also to the racial categories sometimes seen and unchallenged even in white women's travel texts.[5] The prophetic journey, then, was taken with the purpose not only of saving souls but also of changing society.

---

4. By "diverted travel" I mean the discreet strategies employed by blacks to travel from one location to the next because of legalities restricting or forbidding certain blacks, particularly slaves, to travel outside of certain areas. Wearing disguises, hiding out in attics, and passing are examples of the ways in which blacks had to divert attention away from who or where they really were in order to travel safely. The Underground Railroad is probably the best-known mode of diverted travel for blacks. The words *underground* and *railroad* together suggest diverted mobility—that is, movement in "other" directions, out of the sight and attention of whites upholding the fugitive slave laws. Harriet Tubman employed this method of travel both in providing assistance to slaves who were trying to reach several secret Underground Railroad posts and in her own travel north and south to secure more slaves.

5. Sara Mills, in *Discourses of Differences: An Analysis of Women's Travel Writing and Colonialism,* alerts feminists who study the travel texts of white women in the nineteenth century not to forget that the white women travelers were also a part of the very system that they themselves are critiquing (29). This often meant that

The accounts of travel in black religious women's narratives reveal that they felt this obligation within a sociohistorical context in which it was often asserted that as blacks they did not even have souls; that as women, they were neither intelligent nor granted the divine right to convert souls; and that as women, their space was in the private domain, not the public. Logic, then, within this context, would suggest that one without a soul and without right to other people's souls surely cannot convert or save a soul. This logic also suggests that to acquire souls, one had to "go out" to them, and women were not permitted access to that public space. Poststructuralism alerts us that such logic is predicated on binarisms: soul/soulless, man/woman, public/private. The prophetic journey of black religious women inherently challenged such binarisms. In traveling to secure souls for God, black religious women engaged in the very complicated process of exposing such binary elements as constructs, showing the ambiguities and inconsistencies in these constructs, and then expanding or offering alternatives to them.

Despite the fact that during their travels these black religious women endured the "most uncomfortable passages" and were treated "very indifferently indeed" because they were people of color, their prophetic journeying should not be seen as what bell hooks calls "sites of deprivation." Instead, the prophetic journey is closer to what hooks calls a "site of radical possibility, a space of resistance."[6] As mobile women, they were already defying accepted definitions of female behavior by choosing not to stay home to attend to husbands and children. They were traveling, which itself "constitut[ed] a potential breach of the public/private dichotomy" as traveling was an activity generally preserved for men.[7] Moreover, as blacks traveling during the height of slavery, they violated

---

the white women travelers did not challenge their own racist views, which often were revealed in their travel texts in their depictions of blacks and Native Americans. For more on the depictions of blacks and Native Americans in the texts of nineteenth-century travelers, see Ashton Nichols, "Silencing the Other: Discourse of Domination in Nineteenth Century Exploration Narratives"; and Shirley Foster's *Across New Worlds: Nineteenth-Century Women Travellers and Their Writings.*

6. bell hooks, *Yearning: Race, Gender, and Cultural Politics,* 149. hooks argues that despite their historically peripheral status, blacks have been able to use that space on the margins in empowering, self-inventing ways. Black religious women, as hooks notes further, are able to use the margins to "imagine alternatives" (150); ibid., 149.

7. Patricia Cline Cohen, *A Calculating People: The Spread of Numeracy in Early America,* 110.

other social practices and constantly faced the possibilities of immobility and enslavement. Fugitive slave laws permitting slaveholders to search for runaways in the North or the South and the increased number of kidnappings of "free" blacks to enslave them were frightening realities for blacks traveling in the nineteenth century.[8] Most significantly, as people proclaiming their religious authority to preach, these women were traveling to various cities to speak and preach to various audiences from the pulpit, a very masculine and racialized space as well. Indeed, the act of preaching itself defied perceptions of blacks as spiritually and intellectually incapacitated. Traveling on the margins of actual modes of transportation and on the margins of ideologies became for these black women preachers a "central location for the production of counter hegemonic discourse."[9]

To illuminate the terms of this discourse, I discuss the prophetic journeying of black women preachers, mainly Julia Foote and Jarena Lee, from metaphorical, literal, and imperial perspectives. By *metaphorical,* I mean the significance that travel takes for these women in terms of spiritual and personal development. Travel becomes a metaphor for discipleship, of living up to their commands as disciples of God, which in turn is interpreted as self-improvement. Discussing the metaphorical significance of travel foregrounds the factors that propelled their travels. Their knowing why they were traveling demonstrates how religious conviction became a passport for "exercis[ing] personal libert[ies] otherwise unavailable to them as Blacks and as women in the nineteenth century."[10] By *literal* travel, I mean the actual logistics and complications of travel brought about by race, gender, and class ideologies: the close encounters with slavery that they experienced; the long stationary moments they endured because of laws prohibiting blacks to ride with whites; the opposition they encountered as women traveling. Analyzing their travels from this perspective gives insight into the ways in which prophesying daughters used religious conviction as a "compass" with

8. One glaring example of impact of these laws is dealt with in Toni Morrison's *Beloved,* which poignantly fictionalizes the real life of Margaret Garner, an escaped slave who attempts to murder her children when she sees slave catchers coming to return her to slavery.

9. hooks, *Yearning,* 149.

10. Joycelyn Moody, "On the Road with God: Travel and Quest in Early Nineteenth-Century African American Holy Women's Narratives" 38.

which to "chart" their own identities against the backdrop of such social realities as they mapped out new definitions of race and gender. Finally, I will consider how, despite their own challenge to and deconstruction of the ideologies that affect them, they participated in the imperialist act of "othering" as they converted the recalcitrant and the Native American to their religion. Discussing the issue of travel from this perspective does not undermine the prophetic nature of their journeys but instead provides space to consider the complicated nature of their identity, especially as we analyze how they negotiated aspects of their subjectivity that replicated those of the very system against which they were protesting.

As Christians, prophesying daughters first saw their need to travel as a way to fulfill their obligation to God to go and spread His Word. They saw travel as a metaphor for a journey or quest toward spiritual development. As long as they were traveling as "doers of the Word" to please God and to fulfill their duties to Him, they felt as if they were bettering themselves spiritually. Joanne Braxton indicates the metaphorical significance of travel to the development of the spirit by asserting that the purpose of the journey motif in their texts is not "to seek a dignified and self defining identity" but rather to "focus almost wholly on spiritual matters," those matters which please God. Furthermore, William Andrews says that the travel motif "symbolizes multiple layers of spiritual evolution," suggesting that the path toward spiritual development is a continual, ongoing process.[11] The conversion experience that these women went through thus marks the initial step on an extended journey toward spiritual development, in the movement from spiritual vacancy to spiritual awareness. Actual geographic travel becomes important because it correlates to continued spiritual growth, while static moments—when they were unable to travel—correlate to feelings of spiritual dissatisfaction. Conflating the metaphorical spiritual journeying with literal travel, women itinerant preachers experienced spiritual malaise and depression when forced to stay put and relief when they were able to get out and about. Jarena Lee expresses this feeling of malaise when she writes: "I have not traveled so largely, and in this . . . I felt somewhat oppressed" (*Experience*, 46). After having been stationary in Philadelphia for a few weeks,

11. Braxton, *Black Women Writing Autobiography*, 55; Andrews, *Sisters of the Spirit*, 7.

she notes that "my mind became oppressed and I craved to travel" (*Experience*, 80). But when she was able to move after a static period, Jarena Lee says that she "preached three or four times, and found considerable consolation" (*Experience,* 80). Julia Foote had delayed travel for a few years because of an illness, and she felt this inability to travel had an impact on her spirituality: "During all this time I was less spiritual, less zealous" (*Brand,* 80). Traveling, then—the act of moving and engaging in God's work—eased and remedied feelings of spiritual ineptness and depression.

The journey motif also represents for these women a way of fulfilling their roles as disciples or apostles of God. Sue Houchins states that as people called by God to do His Work, these prophesying daughters "model[ed] their lives after the apostles"—those chosen by Jesus during his reign on Earth to travel with him to promulgate his message. Like the apostles, "these women took seriously Christ's command to go empty handed into the world to spread the Gospel."[12] The apostolic significance of the travel motif influenced their interpretation of the social and physical hardships they encountered during their travels. The opposition to women preaching, discrimination on various modes of transportation, and other sociological threats of immobility that Lee and Foote encountered were seen as adversities they had to endure in their path toward spiritual fulfillment. The physical hardships—rough boat rides, jarring road trips, and the laborious and arduous trips that they took by foot for miles in the snow and rain—were seen as further evidence of the extremes they would go through to please God and to attain spiritual satisfaction. Lee, for example, describes one of her journeys as "a very uncomfortable passage" in which she was "very sea-sick indeed" (*Experience,* 45). On another occasion, she indicates that she "walked twenty one miles and preached with difficulty to a stiff-necked and rebellious people"(23). In describing one of her trips, Foote emphasizes that "I was very sick on the journey" (*Brand,* 101). These tribulations were metaphoric tests of spiritual authenticity. Lee felt that, like gold being tested in fire for its purity, "We have to be tried as gold in the fire" (*Experience,* 53).

The metaphoric significance of travel as quest for fulfillment of divine obligation also necessitated confronting, challenging, and changing re-

12. Sue Houchins, introduction to *Spiritual Narratives,* xl.

strictive constructs around race and gender. During the nineteenth century, women's social mobility was limited by the ideology of the cult of true womanhood, which located women's social sphere in the "home." "No woman," as Joycelyn Moody notes, "was at liberty to leave home without arousing suspicion." Because of "societal expectations and cultural norms, domesticity bound essentially all women to the hearth."[13] Articles, books, and other literature aimed at (but not limited to) a black audience reinforced and glorified the image of woman in the home. For instance, the January 26, 1861, edition of the *Christian Recorder* reprinted Lydia H. Sigourney's article "Home," which states that

> . . . the life of woman is in the heart.
>   The smile, the sweet voice, the kind word, the self-forgetful services of love, these are the home. . . . Obeying the injunction of the eloquent apostle, to "learn to show piety at home," may our earthly dwelling place foreshadow that object of our highest aspiration. (7)[14]

Another article in the *Christian Recorder*'s June 8, 1861, issue, "Woman and Home," states that "the social well-being of society rests on our homes, and what are the foundations of our homes but woman's care and devotion?" Both of these statements set up home as a fixed location or "dwelling place" that "woman" must maintain. Emphasizing that the "foundations of our homes" are determined by "woman's care and devotion" further establishes its fixity. It is from this "static" site that the "social well-being of society" was to be shaped. As Christian women, some black women preachers initially tried to adhere to these ideas, but they soon experienced conflict, as the responsibility of being a prophesying daughter meant rejecting domestic responsibility and this restrictive

13. Moody, "On the Road with God," 37.
14. Lydia Huntley Sigourney was a white woman whose writings were very pious and evangelical. Her work particularly appealed to a large female audience and fits within the sentimental tradition of many white women writers of this time period. That the black-owned *Christian Recorder* would reprint Sigourney's views on the role of women shows spaces where the values and gender roles of free blacks often replicated those of mainstream whites. Many black women were bound by these values. For more on the conflict that many black women faced in early black institutions that reinscribed white middle-class values onto them, see James Oliver Horton, *Free People of Color: Inside the African American Community.* See also Gerda Lerner, ed., *Black Women in White America: A Documentary History.*

space. It would be hard to manage a traditional home on the road. Julia Foote's husband, for example, thought that the idea of his wife traveling to preach was "annoying" and "crazy." According to Foote, "He began to speak against it. He said that . . . if I did not stop he would send me back home or to a crazy house" (*Brand,* 59). Her behavior was "crazy" to her husband because it signaled an attempt to cross social boundaries and threatened his patriarchal position in their marriage. For a long time, Foote was forced to suppress her desires to prophesy and travel because of her husband's objections.

Jarena Lee was immobilized as well by her responsibility to her husband, who was a minister. When her husband was appointed to another church outside of Philadelphia, she had to leave her established position as an exhorter (a church member who expounds on scriptures and lessons but is not considered a preacher). Living up to gender expectations, Lee considered her obligation to her husband primary to everything else. According to Lee, "it became necessary, therefore, for me to remove" (*Experience,* 13). But while there with her husband, she recalls often feeling "discontented" and "afflicted" from being bound within domestic borders. Later, with the absence of both their husbands (Lee's husband had died, and Foote's husband had left on a navy expedition) and the domination they represented, Lee and Foote began to travel and refused to be restricted again.

It could be argued that they still conformed to traditional notions of womanhood because they didn't begin to travel extensively until symbols of patriarchy in their lives were erased. Yet their initial apprehension about striking out on their own and their compliance with gendered norms are understandable. Their conflict about becoming itinerant preachers demonstrates the uneasy meeting of secular and religious expectations, especially since they felt they had been instructed by God to cross traditional boundaries. In a sense, they occupied a divine/secular contact zone, a social space where—to amend Mary Louis Pratt's description of cultural contact zones—secular and divine expectations meet, clash, and grapple with each other.[15] In this zone, the relations to domination and subordination are inverted because divine injunctions take precedence over cultural tradition. The women's initial compliance

15. Mary Louise Pratt, *Imperial Eyes: Travel Writing and Transculturalism,* 4.

with this norm was a part of the grappling process; eventually, however, they complied with God's expectations regardless of opposition they encountered, even opposition within their own institutions.

Black institutions such as the African Methodist Episcopal Church— with which many black women preachers were affiliated—made clear what constituted "proper" female behavior. Such notions were reinforced in their newspapers and other forms of expression, which sent the message to black women that women were supposed to be pure, gentle, loving, sensitive, caring, and domestic. James Oliver Horton points us to an article in the 1839 edition of the *Colored American* magazine that "laid out the differences between men and women in clear and comparative terms":

> Man is strong—Woman is beautiful
> Man is daring and confident—Woman is deferent and unassuming
> Man is great in action—Woman is suffering
> Man shines abroad—Woman at home
> Man talks to convince—Woman to persuade and please
> Man has a rugged heart—Woman has a soft and tender one
> Man prevents misery—Woman relieves it
> Man has science—Woman has taste
> Man has judgment—Woman has sensibility
> Man is a being of justice—Woman is an angel of mercy.[16]

Such social guidelines created an interesting dilemma. As prophesying daughters, the terms used to describe male behavior applied directly to them. As women going against the grain, they were extremely "strong" and "daring and confident." As traveling women, they were "shining abroad" and not at home. As preachers and speakers, they "talked to convince" people to change their social and moral ways. They also used the Word of God to "prevent misery." They exercised profound judgment. They were "beings of justice" as they spoke out against the injustices they encountered at the hands of those opposing their actions.

Despite the challenges to such guidelines that their continued travel signaled, and despite their blurring the boundaries between the above-mentioned binaries, prophesying daughters still had their own ideas of gender deportment during their travels—how they should act and

16. Horton, *Free People of Color*, 102–3.

appear in public. To them, there was a womanly way to be unwomanly. This contradictory act of behaving like a woman even as you did not created another alternative narrative space.

This is seen particularly in the alternative childcare arrangements that Jarena Lee made for her children. Since she was engaged in prophetic journeying, how she took care of children had to be nontraditional in the nineteenth-century sense. She created a system of networking that allowed her flexibility to travel. Parents, friends, and church members kept her child while she traveled. She had such confidence in their care of her child and such dedication to traveling for God that she notes at one point that while away for a week, "not one thought of my little son came into my mind; it was hid from me, lest I should have been diverted from the work I had to do, to look after my son. . . . I now returned home, found all well; no harm had come to my child, although it was very sick. Friends had taken care of it which was of the Lord (*Experience*, 18). This shows that even though she struggled internally with having to leave her child for such long periods in the care of others, she continued to travel extensively. The longest period she records being away from her child was two-and-a-half years. During this time, she left him with Richard Allen, the bishop of the African Methodist Episcopal Church. Lee states that "after being absent for two years and six months, I found Bishop Allen in very ill health, but he ever continued with unwearied interest in my son's welfare, by sending him to school and otherwise improving him in education" (*Experience*, 61).

Nineteenth-century ideologies about motherhood constantly emphasized that women should stay home and devote themselves wholeheartedly to the care of their children. Lee's decision to travel meant rejecting those ideals altogether. Allen died within a few months of Lee's return, and she was faced with the issue of who would provide care for her child while she continued to travel. She found a replacement instantly: "immediately afterwards, I placed my son with a French gentleman, with whom he stayed and learned the cabinet-making business" (*Experience*, 61). For her, traditional motherhood became secondary to her call to travel for God's purpose. Consequently, she relied on other means of providing care for them. She obviously placed her children in the care of respectable community members who would offer her children the attention and nurturing that she could not while she was on the road.

Instead of acquiescing to the immobility encoded in society's delin-
eation of her responsibility to her children, Lee continued to travel. In
doing so, she redefined motherhood in relation to her religious obliga-
tions. Motherhood to her did not mean staying home to attend to every
need of her children. Instead, it meant doing what she needed to for
God, knowing that whether she was home or not, He would provide
them with their needs. Lee believed "that she was liberated from . . . the
expectations of her culture by God who was the highest authority." This
liberation allowed her to reject cultural norms and to transcend identities as dependent wife and mother.[17] Free of domestic restrictions, Lee
became serious about "breaking up housekeeping and forsaking all to
preach the everlasting gospel" (*Experience*, 18).

"Forsaking all" to travel and preach God's Word necessitated the construction of a new "home." For women on the road, home becomes the
geographical area that they cover in their travels—an area that, according to Lee, "would stretch from one end of the earth to the other" (*Experience,* 30). Home, then, is not a fixed location; rather, it is mobile,
with shifting boundaries that are determined by the movements of the
traveler: "[H]ome is no longer just one place. It is locations."[18] By "forsaking all" to travel, prophesying daughters destabilized the "foundation" of traditional homesites, negotiating and recreating the contours
of the space out of which they also had to construct new identities for
themselves.

This new home is mobile in two ways. First, because prophesying
daughters took their new ideas of home and womanhood with them
wherever they went—whether alone or on the decks of boats or in stagecoaches—the mobility that their presence implied signaled an overt
challenge to a static domestic space. Thus their movements helped to
construct a new idea of what constitutes home. Second, home is mobile
because of its propensity to expand. Each new place visited and each
person converted expands the dimensions of home, the site where these
women preachers experienced feelings of belonging and comfort. Many
of these sites of comfort were in what Victor Turner calls liminal, or
"outsider," spaces. Carla Peterson notes that for black women, and especially prophesying daughters, "these liminal spaces came to function as

17. Barbara MacHaffie, *Her Story: Women in Christian Tradition,* 35.
18. hooks, *Yearning,* 148.

their 'center,' offering them greater possibilities of self expression as well as the potential to effect social change."[19] For these women, these liminal spaces were bush clearings, private homes, meeting halls, and tents.

bell hooks has suggested that the domestic space for black women historically has been a site of resistance for them, a space where they can exercise control away from the outside forces of hegemony. According to hooks, "it has been primarily the responsibility of black women to construct domestic households as spaces of care and nurturance in the face of the brutal harsh reality of racist oppression, of sexist domination. Historically, African-American people believed that the construction of a homeplace, however fragile and tenuous, had a radical political dimension."[20]

Whereas many black women have appropriated the home as a site of self-definition, self-empowerment, and even political empowerment, the prophetic journeying of black women preachers called into question the idea of homespace as the site of care and nurturing usually provided by women. Foote and Lee saw their designations as nurturers and caretakers as limitations to their obligation to God. The nature of their work made exercising power within their immediate domestic space counterproductive to their need to reach many people and impact society. Self-recovery, self-definition, and self-construction for them were to derive meaning from spaces outside of the domestic homeplace. As mobile women, they needed to "expand the circumference of the 'woman's sphere' beyond the home to its surrounding environs."[21]

This expansion of the terms of *home* and *women's sphere* explains what appears to be a preoccupation with travel, the prophesying daughters' propensity to chart not only the places to which they traveled but also the number of miles they covered. Lee felt it necessary to indicate at one point in her text that "I have travelled two hundred and eleven miles and preached the Kingdom of God" (*Experience,* 51). One year, she "travelled two thousand three hundred and twenty-five miles and preached one hundred and seventy-eight sermons" (*Experience,* 51). She also records that "in the year of 1835, I travelled 721 miles, and preached 692 sermons. . . . In 1836, I travelled 556 miles and preached 111 sermons" (*Ex-*

---

19. Peterson, *Doers of the Word,* 17–18.
20. hooks, *Yearning,* 42.
21. Moody, "On the Road with God," 37.

perience, 77). At one point, Foote indicates that in one year she "visited too large a number of places to mention in this little booklet" (*Brand,* 92). By indicating the number of miles traveled and sermons preached, they also chart new identities. As Theodore Sarbin suggests, the "place identity" that these women map out in their travels "is an intregral part of the self" they reconstruct, a self more aligned with their spiritual calling than with domestic duties.[22] Moreover, their legitimacy and commitment to God are revealed in their accounts of the miles traveled and the lives they touched with their sermons.

The space of the newly defined home that these prophesying daughters constructed has temporal ramifications as well, as seen in the way in which they constructed this space so that it could expand beyond their time period into that of any reader. In a sense, the word, or the text, "travels." They knew that the written word could reach far more people than they actually could in their own physical travels. The written, published word gave them a sense of continuity. Jarena Lee says to her reader: "Dear reader . . . Though I may never see you in the flesh, I leave on this page my solemn entreaty that you delay not to obtain the pardoning favor of God; . . . **but now, even now**, seek the Lord with full purpose of heart, and He will be fond of thee" (*Experience,* 31; my emphasis). Lee figures that the "now" transforms the moment that she was writing the text into whatever moment or time period in which the reader is reading her text. At whatever "time" the reader encounters Lee's text, she is still able to encourage her or him to convert, thus attempting to further expand the notion of home. This is why Lee states her hope that her text "may at some future day be published. But for the satisfaction of such as may follow after me, when I am no more, I have recorded how the Lord called me to his work" (*Experience,* 97). The written word, which recorded her "work" for God, continues to play a role in her prophetic journey as it extends beyond her own historical moment, "when [she] is no more." She is gone, but her words live on.

But while she was alive and well and was rejecting the constraints of home and domesticity, Lee and other prophesying daughters still had to contend with codes of gender behavior that existed on modes of transportation during her day. Patricia Cline Cohen notes that because of the

22. Theodore Sarbin, "Place Identity as a Component of Self: An Addendum," 1.

serious danger that women could encounter while traveling, they were expected to comply with cultural expectations of proper behavior.[23] In addition to dressing conservatively and avoiding being too friendly with strangers, this often meant having a female companion. Throughout their texts, Lee and Foote make constant reference to various women who traveled with them. Lee speaks affectionately of Sister Mary Owen, noting that on several occasions, Owen, "who had laid aside all the cares of the world, went with me" (*Experience,* 72). She also mentions a Jane Hutt; another woman, whom Lee identifies only with initials; and several other women, to whom she refers as either "a good sister" or "sister."

Julia Foote mentions women traveling with her but notes that often "a very dear sister, Ann M. Johnson, accompanied me." In fact, she references Johnson four times in the book, mentioning her praying, singing, and sharing her religious experiences with their audiences. Foote also includes the following commentary on her death: "In 1856, Sister Johnson, who had been my companion during all these years of travel, left me for her heavenly home. She bore her short illness without a murmur, resting on Jesus. As she lived, so she died, in the full assurance of faith, happy and collected to the last" (*Brand,* 110).

Whether traveling with partners or alone, the prophetic journeying of prophesying daughters positioned them very well to question how race figured into gendered travel behavior. Although Cohen does briefly discuss class dynamics on the public transportation system, indicating how lower-class women complicated the temporary space that the "respectable" women had managed to obtain, Cohen does not factor in how race figured into gendered travel behavior. Race and class forced black women preachers out of codes around gender and threatened their mobility. "Femaleness" while traveling seemed primarily associated with whiteness. Race many times ruled out any rights or expectations accorded white women. This is such a prevailing factor that Foote devotes an entire chapter in her autobiography to "indignities on account of color."

Foote describes an incident that exemplifies this dilemma, in which a white man who could not find a cabin in the male quarters threatened to remove her from the ladies' section of a train. Upon finding Foote in the

23. Cohen, *A Calculating People,* 110–11.

cabin, he vehemently exclaimed that "that nigger has no business here. My family are coming on board . . . , and they shall not come where a nigger is" (*Brand*, 91). Foote's presence on the train apparently symbolized an intrusion into this man's space. His anger does not appear to be directed at the fact that she is female but that she is a "nigger." Foote protests his attack on her color. She states further that "they called the captain, and he ordered me to get up; but I did not stir, thinking it best not to leave the bed except by force" (*Brand*, 91). Her refusal to get up illustrates her conscious effort not to allow social constructs of race to immobilize her.

Foote explains another incident where her presence on public transportation "during her travels for the Lord" impinged on white male public space. She encountered one man traveling alone with her in a stagecoach who "seemed very uneasy" about traveling next to a black woman (*Brand*, 91). Foote states that "at each stopping place, he would say: 'I am afraid the public will take me for an abolitionist today'" (*Brand*, 91). This fear of how he would be perceived by others is a result more of her race than her gender. People would not immediately associate his traveling with a white woman with the abolitionist movement. Foote notes that by acting uneasy and by making such a statement, this man was "showing his dark, slave holding principles" to which she is opposed (*Brand*, 91).

Foote's presence in the ladies' cabin and in the stagecoach with this man may suggest that black women had ready access to modes of transportation. This certainly was not the case. As indicated earlier, black women often had to travel on decks or in mail coaches. At other times, their travel would be delayed if whites objected to traveling in the presence of blacks. Foote recounts such an incident where she had to put off traveling for four days because of objections to her presence: "We were not permitted to leave until four days afterwards. At that time a colored person was not allowed to ride in the stage if any white passenger objected to it. There were objections made for three mornings, but, on the fourth, the stage called for us and we had a safe journey" (*Brand*, 108). In this case, race resulted in actual immobility.

That such immobility was a reality for blacks traveling during the nineteenth century is demonstrated by the fact that the *Christian Recorder* often provided information and announcements that warned blacks of dangers of traveling. For instance, the February 23, 1861, edition issued a warning to blacks traveling south: "We give notice to all our people who are in the habit of going South, to Baltimore and Washington, that the way is hedged up between here and there. No colored person is allowed to pass Havre de Grace, but is taken from cars, fined $20, and then made to return from whence they came. Quite a number, lately, have been stopped, fined, and turned back."

The *Recorder* also kept black travelers informed about accidents and other dangers while traveling. For example, the February 9, 1861, edition placed this announcement concerning the safety of travel: "**Safe Traveling.**—By railway accidents in 1860, there were killed, in the United States, seventy-four persons, and three hundred and fifteen were wounded—the smallest number in any twelve months in the past eight years." The *Recorder* also made information on boarding available to black travelers. One such announcement in the June 21, 1862, edition reads: "**Boarding**. We call special attention to the advertisement of Mrs. Plant's Boarding House, located in Brooklyn, New York—No. 197 High St. We . . . can recommend her establishment to all those who go to New York with the intention of remaining a few days."

Lee and Foote continued to travel to the South despite the dangers and threats to their lives. Foote describes an incident that occurred to her in Baltimore, where she could have been enslaved: "Upon our arrival there we were closely examined for marks on our persons by which to identify us if we should prove to be run-aways. . . . They repeated this for several nights. They often came to our bed and held their light in our faces to see if one for whom they were looking was not with us" (*Brand,* 99).

While traveling, these women were always exposed to this kind of uncertainty that could instantly either end or alter their travel plans. Marilyn Wesley's analysis of what she calls "haphazard movement" in the captivity narrative of Mary Rowlandson proves useful in understanding the volatility to which prophesying daughters were constantly exposed because of social codes and legalities. Held captive by Native Americans, Rowlandson describes how often on the spur of the moment, she and the other prisoners would be forced by their captors to change their course of travel. These sudden changes in direction, according to Wesley, were strategic moves on the part of the Native Americans, but Rowlandson represented them as erratic. Wesley describes this seemingly arbitrary change of travel as "haphazard movement." The uncertainty that Rowlandson described feeling as the Indians directed her movement may be similar to the uncertainty that prophesying daughters felt with their movements directed by white Americans in the nineteenth century.

Despite the threats that race and gender imposed on their travels, these women, as Jarena Lee states, "felt it [their] duty to travel up and down in the world, and promulgate the gospel of Christ" (*Experience,* 30). This travel to fulfill their divine duties and to assert Christian values was certainly not without problems. Their travel with the intent of "converting" people to Christianity suggests the existence of a binary as to what is or is not Christian, a presupposition that made these women preachers very prone to the act of "othering." Those who were unconverted and unsaved were seen as the "other" from their perspective. Any behavior exhibited by those they intended to convert that did not conform to their perception of how Christians should behave was interpreted in such a way as to legitimate their attempts to convert them. For instance, Lee used such words as "cruel," "obdurate," "unholy," and "mean" to describe nonbelievers. Although Lee also uses a lot of these words to describe people she encountered whose behavior toward her was racist or sexist, this racist and sexist behavior provided further testimony to the need of conversion.

One of the most noticeable places where this othering is seen is in the depiction of the "Indian" (Native American) as wild, heathenistic, and savage. For instance, another prophesying daughter, Maria Stewart, in trying to argue for black nationhood, discusses how various nations have distinguished themselves. She asserts that despite various initial weaknesses, these nations proved themselves great. She uses a term that describes the negative prenation state of these groups followed by positive, affirmative adjectives to describe the nations after they asserted themselves and acquired nationhood. According to Stewart, though the Greeks were "suffering" at first, they became "united, and came off victorious" (*Productions,* 61). The "Haytians," she noted, were unacknowledged (*Productions,* 61) but had a "firmness of character" that was "admirable" (*Productions,* 61). She further states that the Poles were at first "feeble," but that they rose to be "gallant" (*Productions,* 61). Though she says that the Indians as a nation are "united," she describes them as "the wild Indians of the forest." The terms used to describe the other nations' prenation state point to their conditions as being imposed by opposing forces—forces that make them "suffer," or "feeble," or "unacknowledged." But "wild" suggests a characteristic intrinsic to the Indians that sets them apart from others. And placing them in "the forest" sets them apart because it suggests primitivism and an absence of civilization. This objectification of the Indian suggests that during their travels these women had some sense of cultural superiority to the Indian.

Lee provides another example of how the Indian is "othered." Describing one of her visits to an Indian camp, Lee notes that

> I could not help admiring the ways of the children. The teachers bring them up in one English language and dress some of them in the English style, but the greatest number are clad in the Indian style; those of the old Indians in their blankets. . . . It was in the month of March—it rained and snowed—yet they walked in their moccasins, and some bareheaded—. . . . Much weeping among them, dear reader, take notice, not withstanding they are a nation revolted from Israel, and would not be governed. Yet they can be civilized and Christianized. We might call them heathens, but they are endowed with a Christian spirit. (*Experience,* 51)

Nowhere else in her text does Lee give such a detailed description of the clothes and physical appearances of people she encounters. Lee offers idealized, stereotypical depictions of these Indians in moccasins or as bareheaded to show the contrast between their style and the English style. This contrast depicts a "difference" intended to testify to the need of Christianizing or converting these Indians. Lee is also asserting that although they have been a "revolted nation," the weeping and crying they were doing upon hearing her sermon are indications of inclinations to be "saved." Display of this kind of emotion signifies a Christian spirituality, which is why she makes the statement, "yet they can be civilized and Christianized." Such terms suggest preconceived standards for what constitutes being civilized, standards that the Indians do not meet. These preachers dismiss the legitimacy of Indian culture and the Indians' right to their own practices regardless of how "other-like" they appear, and the preachers set out to "save" them. For some modern readers, this poses a serious contradiction. On the one hand, these women's own travel to expand the kingdom of God complicated and challenged notions of race, class, and gender as seen in their (de)(re)construction of femininity and in their rejections of racial constructs. On the other hand, however, they tended to re-inscribe and re-institute some of the similar "othering" behavior prevalent in American society during the nineteenth century. Their social marginalization as blacks and as women did not rule out their propensity to accept the dominant discourse that regarded the Native American as savage and uncivilized.

This contradiction may be less problematic if one recognizes the perceptions and intent that underlay the way these women preachers approached the conversion of Indians. As the prophesying daughters viewed their travels from a spiritual perspective, race was not an issue to them. They saw the Indians—as they saw everyone else they encountered—as souls that needed to be converted over to Christ. This is why Lee is able to say "we might call them heathens, but they are endowed with a Christian spirit." This heathen/nonheathen binary was set up not to elevate themselves but rather as a way to elevate God.

The travel accounts of black women preachers add a different dimension to the social landscape of nineteenth-century America. They reveal these women consciously interjecting themselves in the landscape, consequently altering it. Their travels depict women defining themselves in terms of spiritual development. They reveal a journey from silence encoded in domesticity to vocality, as seen in their reshaping of the domestic sphere to extend far beyond the traditional home. This vocality is seen also in narrations of their refusals of the race and class constructs that infringed on their determination to live up to their call to spread God's Word.

FIVE

Prophetic Reading

BLACK WOMEN PREACHERS AND
BIBLICAL INTERPRETATION

In 1855, while in Geneva, New York, one of the many locations she was to visit that year to preach, Julia Foote met with several "sisters" of the Methodist Church to form a moral reform society. Moral reform and missionary societies were becoming very prevalent in the nineteenth century among black women. Many women, usually affiliated with churches, banded together and organized groups that would visit the sick, provide clothing and shelter for the homeless, and perform other benevolent acts. Not only did these organizations serve as sites for networking, building sisterly relations, and socializing, they also "transformed unknown and unconfident women into leaders and agents of social service and racial self help in their communities."[1]

As Foote left this particular moral reform meeting, church officials extended her an invitation to preach at the church the following evening. This offer, however, was met later with vehement protest. A minister by the name of Mr. Monroe, and another man, whom Foote labels "a fiend in human shape," boldly insisted that they would not allow Foote to preach in the church because "they did not believe in women's preaching, and would not admit one in the church" (*Brand*, 87). The minister continued his protest, telling Foote that the only way she could have access to the pulpit would be if "they break my head." To this, Foote responded, "God can take you from the pulpit without breaking your head," at which point the minister "raved as if he were a mad man"

---

1. Higginbotham, *Righteous Discontent*, 17.

(*Brand*, 88). Foote notes that during this confrontation, the men attempted to legitimate their protest, "striving hard to justify themselves from the Bible," which one was holding in what Foote describes as "unholy hands" (*Brand*, 88).

This preacher's holding up the Bible was a symbolic gesture intended to signify that the Bible supported and substantiated his protest against women preaching. Such Bible-based discourse represents one of the most serious points of contention facing black women preachers in the nineteenth century. Julia Foote, Jarena Lee, Maria Stewart, and Frances Gaudet were called to preach in a cultural context where identifications of gender were being created, prescribed, and maintained based on the Bible. As long as Foote was meeting with the women of the church to carry out the domestic function of forming a moral reform society, there seems to have been no protest. I do not intend to undermine the significance of moral reform societies and the vital role that women played in them. That black church women organized, raised funds, and carried out various functions within these societies has been interpreted by scholars such as Cheryl Townsend Gilkes, Jualyne Dodson, and others as illustrating that women were able to attain power positions. What I am arguing here is that men in the church were not threatened by women's participation in such ventures because the moral reform societies did not threaten to remove power over the organizational structure of the church from men's hands. Having women preach, on the other hand, did pose a threat to men's organizational power, because preaching brought with it the authority and public visibility generally associated with masculinity. As Minister Monroe's actions indicate, this was not a role that men were willing to give up readily. So when Foote ventured out to cross the gender divide and dared to preach, there ensued, to use Foote's term, "pandemonium."

In the midst of this pandemonium, the preacher summoned the Bible as a referee. Minister Monroe's lifting the Bible above his head symbolized its elevated status in nineteenth-century society. It was considered to hold unquestionable truths, and among those "truths" was the role of women in society. That he was so vehement and belligerent indicates that Foote's desire to preach undermined these constructions of status and truth, causing him to rave "as if he were a mad man." The notions of gendered behavior that were allegedly supported by the Bible—and to which Foote's preaching was posing a threat—are rooted in the nineteenth-century "cult of true womanhood," in which a woman's role, as spelled out by feminist historian Barbara Welter, was to practice piety, purity, virtue, submission, and family devotion. Though Foote was affiliated with the African Methodist Episcopal Church, she still had to contend with nineteenth-century notions of gender, as black institutions like the church adopted mainstream society's views about the position of women. Several passages from the Bible frequently were being used then to justify this gendered behavior.[2] So the minister is most likely referring to the often-cited biblical passage from 1 Corinthians 14:34–35: "Let your women keep silent in the churches, for they are not permitted to speak, but they are to be submissive, as the law also says. And if they want to learn something, let them ask their own husbands at home."

As the passage replicates almost exactly the tenets of the cult of true womanhood, it is understandable why it was often cited. Claiming that the Bible mandated that women "not be permitted to speak" substantiated the nineteenth-century notion that women should remain in the private space of the home and stay away from the masculine public space represented in arenas such as politics and the pulpit where vocality was essential. The biblical assertion that "they are to be submissive" maintains the established male title as head of the household to whom woman is to acquiesce. This assertion also reemphasized the notion that a woman truly devoted to her husband and children should surrender her own needs and desires to theirs.

The minister was most likely referencing other concepts based in biblical scripture like those projected by Stephen Knowlton in "The Silence of Women in the Churches." Barbara Zikmund points us to his article, which appears in the 1867 edition of the *Congregational Quarterly.* Even though this article appeared a few years after Foote's text, it still represents the kind of thought that confronted Foote and other women preachers. Knowlton's article asserts that the Bible itself substantiates woman's natural inferiority to man. He states that women's position in the order of creation and their weakness in the creation of mankind are proof of their divinely mandated subservient position. Being created after man, woman must accept her secondary position. Also, according

2. For more discussion of this idea and how women responded, see C. Eric Lincoln and Lawrence H. Mamiya, *The Black Church in the African American Experience.* See also Cheryl Townsend Gilkes, "The Politics of 'Silence': Dual-Sex Political Systems and Women's Traditions of Conflict in African-American Religion."

to Knowlton, by persuading Adam (man) to partake of fruit forbidden him by God, woman proved her inherent weakness. Knowlton states that "this implies that woman, having taken the lead once, and made such bad work of it, there is a special fitness that she hereafter march in the rear. She made a little speech once that was the world's undoing: now let her keep silence."[3] Woman's "silence," then, according to Knowlton's discourse, was a result of "her" own doing in the Bible. How women were to behave in the nineteenth century was merely a historical "working out" of punishment for her actions. This is the context of biblical interpretation, then, into which black women preachers were called to preach in the nineteenth century, and Minister Monroe's holding up the Bible was a reminder of this.

As blacks, these women were already familiar with the biblical injunctions that were employed to substantiate racial ideologies. The authority of the Bible was used to frame blacks as culturally inferior in order to justify holding them in social and physical bondage. Katie Cannon provides summaries of Bible-based mythologies and ideologies constructed to frame blacks in ways that justified their physical and social enslavement. For example, the Bible—specifically the story of Ham in Genesis 9:25–27—was used to validate as an act of God the enslavement of blacks and their assignment to subservient roles.[4] Blacks, as the "darker" race, were to identify as descendants of this curse and accept their socially inferior position as slaves or as inheritors of the slavery tradition.

Despite this use of the Bible, blacks generally continued to use it as a source of self-understanding and liberation, a feat that continues to this day. It is a feat that has inspired black and feminist scholars to posit a distinct African American religion and hermeneutic.[5] Katie Cannon, for example, notes elsewhere that, "In spite of the distortions and misinterpretations by racists, Black folks have never ceased in their task to discern the real biblical message of liberation and wholeness. Heroically,

3. Zikmund, "Biblical Arguments and Women's Place in the Church" 332.
4. Katie Cannon, "Slave Ideology and Biblical Interpretation," 11.
5. There are various excellent works on how blacks' relationship with the Bible shaped and sustained African American religion. In addition to works by Katie Cannon, see, for example, Albert Raboteau, *Slave Religion: The "Invisible Institution" in the Antebellum South*; Mechal Sobel, *Trabelin' On: The Slave Journey to an Afro-Baptist Faith*; Howard Thurman, *Jesus and the Disinherited*; and James Cone, *For My People: Black Theology and the Black Church*.

they have resisted reducing the Bible to just another tool in the hands of their oppressors." Similarly, Cain Felder argues that in spite of the various forms of oppression that the Bible was used to legitimate, "biblical stories, themes, personalities and images have inspired, captivated, given meaning, and served as a basis of hope for a liberated and thus enhanced material life for Blacks in America."[6]

As women, prophesying daughters had to engage in a similar critical approach to the Bible when confronted with gender-based restrictions that went against the identities they had already formed for themselves. Foote's reaction to the minister's raising the Bible to justify why she could not preach provides an example of how they responded to this conflict. Her contention that the minister was "striving hard to justify [himself] from the Bible" speaks to two key factors at the core of this chapter. First, to say that he was "striving hard" to find in the Bible justification against her preaching suggests that Foote sees that this social reality confronting her was merely a construct. Readings and interpretations of the Bible were not naturally embedded in the Bible itself. Instead, readings of the Bible dictated social realities. Such interpretations, then, were constructs designed and institutionalized to maintain power relations that lowered women's position in the church and society at the same time that they were elevating those in political power. Second, the contention that the preacher was "striving hard" suggests that Foote had her own views and understandings of the Bible, and that the preacher's views apparently did not meet the standards of her interpretations.

Foote and other prophesying women had counterarguments to such hegemonic readings. They provided their own very close textual readings of the Bible based on an interpretative context informed by their race and gender. They shared these readings in their autobiographies, and the result has been alternative readings and uses of the Bible that challenge any notion of a monolithic, "traditional" interpretive approach to the Bible in the nineteenth century. It is from these readings that scholars can begin exploring not only how nineteenth-century black women were critically engaging the world of the Bible as a site of self-understanding, but also how these readings provide further insight into

---

6. Katie Cannon, "The Bible from the Perspective of the Racially and Economically Oppressed," 35; Cain Hope Felder, *Troubling Biblical Waters: Race, Class, and Family,* 156.

the way they appropriated the world of the Bible as a legitimate site to substantiate their demands for social and political equality. By revealing prevalent interpretations of the Bible as mere interpretations not mandated by the text itself, black women preachers used the Bible to open up space for themselves and their listeners to contest the theology that legitimated their own subordination. Revealing dominant interpretations as flawed and illegitimate enabled these women to claim the authority of the Bible for themselves through interpretations that stressed the right and obligation of women to preach.

By questioning the legitimacy of existing social relations and providing a biblical rationale for new ones, they nurtured and sustained radical resistance to oppressive ideologies and practices in the present while preparing themselves and their listeners for the possibility of more radical ones in the future. Much of what these black women preachers were doing in the early part of nineteenth century paved the way for many female preachers at the end and turn of the century, so that by the time we read the autobiographies of women like Frances Joseph Gaudet (1913), we see a more active and visible presence of women preachers. Also, although white women such as Frances Willard and Elizabeth Cady Stanton recognized and refuted the tendency of white men to use religion and biblical arguments to keep women and women preachers out of the pulpit and other public arenas, Stewart made these arguments in print at least twenty years earlier than did Stanton. This strongly suggests that these black prophesying daughters were at the forefront of feminist theology and of the religious activism usually associated with white women.

But the important question now is how Foote and other prophesying daughters were able to provide biblical rationale for their activity, especially when we consider the fact that they continued to preach in a context and from a text that was used to subjugate them. This certainly would seem at first to be an act of self-annihilation, one that contributed to their own oppression. However, it is important to understand the position of the Bible in these women's lives. The Bible was a source they felt they had to fully comprehend. Their interpretations and readings of it made the Bible not only a guide for living and preaching but also a language base from which they articulated their understandings of who they were and the adversities and opposition that they were experiencing as black women preachers in the nineteenth century. They attained this knowledge by reading and rereading the Bible. Julia Foote, for example, says that "I studied the Bible at every spare moment, that I might be able to read it with better understanding" (*Brand*, 35). Stewart states that "it was the book that I mostly studied, and now . . . my heart is most generally meditating upon its divine truths" (*Productions*, 24). They both recognized that their study of the Bible entitled them to their understanding as they saw it. Jarena Lee shared this belief. Feeling that the Holy Spirit guided her to learning the Scriptures, she states, "I have never found that Spirit led me contrary to the Scriptures of truth, as I understand them" (*Experience*, 97).

These understandings, then, were used as the basis for refuting oppressive constructs being legitimated by dominant interpretations of the Bible. From their own interpretative context, black women preachers offered alternative readings to such constructs around gender and race. Julia Foote admits that when confronted with racist or sexist encounters, "I took my Bible and read many of my choice passages" (*Brand*, 46). She chose passages that were particularly relevant to social conditions and circumstances limiting her life in the nineteenth century. Black women preachers brought to the texts of the Bible their experiences as part of a large class of underprivileged, uneducated free blacks; this informed not only their interpretation of the Bible but also their selection of passages to read. In many ways, this selection of "choice" passages was a hermeneutical approach to the Bible practiced by many African Americans who—despite the Bible's use to oppress them—still found relevance, refuge, and solace in it. For example, Howard Thurman reveals that when he would read to his illiterate grandmother, "she was most particular about the choice of Scripture" she wanted read to her.[7] Thurman's grandmother did not particularly want to hear passages from Paul because, according to her:

> [D]uring the days of slavery, the master's minister would occasionally hold services for the slaves. Old man McGhee was so mean that he would not let a Negro minister preach to his slaves. Always the white minister used as his text something about Paul. At least three or four times a year he used as a text: "Slaves, be obedient to them that are your master . . . , as unto Christ." Then he would go on to show how it was God's will that we were slaves and how, if we were good and happy slaves, God would bless

7. Thurman, *Jesus and the Disinherited*, 30.

us. I promised my Maker that if I ever learned to read and if freedom ever came, I would not read that part of the Bible.[8]

Black women preachers used what biblical scholars such as Elizabeth S. Fiorenza and Katie Cannon call the "hermeneutics of suspicion," or "the ability to understand that there is no value free space" and to be "attentive to that which may be wrong or hurtful to the community's well-being." They were critically aware, as was Thurman's grandmother, of the political and socioeconomic factors that influenced the promotion of certain readings or interpretations of the biblical text. The fact that they had "choice passages" not only shows a critical awareness of how the Bible was intended to be used against them, but, as Renita Weems asserts, it also shows that they rejected antagonistic readings that denied them their own definitions of subjectivity.[9] Therefore, many of the "choice passages" depicted people and situations that replicated or reemphasized their own projections of who they were in the nineteenth century. And many of their chosen passages depicted women as assertive figures playing roles other than the "silent" ones that nineteenth-century ideology prescribed. Other choice Bible passages concerned oppressed ethnic groups that were ultimately victorious over their oppressors.

It is instructive to note, before discussing these manipulations for self-affirmation in more detail, that as Christians, prophesying daughters did recognize the Bible's importance as a spiritual source. As preachers, they did indeed perform the nominal interpretations of the Bible, expounding on the Scriptures and pointing out their spiritual and moral relevance to human life. In this sense, black women preachers used and expounded on the Bible as a guide for holy living. For instance, Lee felt that God had sent her, as a woman, "to preach the simple story of the birth, life, death and resurrection of our Lord, and accompany it too with power to the sinner's heart" (*Experience,* 12). She knew that the way to the sinner's heart was to use the Bible to show him the way to live a more holy life. Although she does not provide her complete sermons in the text, she does give summaries of them on occasion. In one in particular, her normative use of the Scriptures is apparent:

8. Ibid., 30–31.
9. Cannon, "The Bible from the Perspective of the Racially and Economically Oppressed," 36–37; Renita Weems, "Reading Her Way through the Struggle: African American Women and the Bible."

> Acts xiii, 41—"Behold ye despisers, and wonder and perish." I pointed
> out the portion of the hypocrite, the liar, the Sabbath-breaker, and all
> who do wickedly and die in their sins; they shall be to the judgment bar
> of Jehovah, and before an assembled universe hear their awful sentence,
> "Depart from me, ye cursed, into everlasting fire, prepared for the devil
> and his angels," while the righteous shall be received "into life eternal."
> (*Experience*, 30)

Here Lee indicates to the audience what will be their plight if they did not
live holy lives as prescribed in the Bible. In another instance, she makes
the same plea to the reader: "Dear Reader, if you have not, I charge you
to make your peace with God while time and opportunity is given. . . .
Seek the Lord with full purpose of heart, and he will be fond of thee"
(*Experience*, 31). Along with Lee, both Foote and Stewart in various di-
gressions in their texts employ this normative use of the Bible as a source
for good and holy living.

The nineteenth century saw many theological debates about the Bible,
such as those concerning the idea of common sense and the Bible; science and the Bible; and the Bible and history. Although black women
did expound on the spiritual significance of the Scriptures, their reality in the nineteenth century did not allow much space for them to be
able to participate fully in such theological debates. Vincent Wimbush
has noted that blacks "as a whole were otherwise disposed during this
period, struggling for basic human rights. Thus, they were hardly in a
position to engage the emergent critical methods." Because of blacks'
struggle for basic rights, Monroe Fordham has also noted that "Black
religious thought has never reflected a primary concern with theological debates and philosophical consideration of religious ideas and concepts within themselves."[10] This also applies to black women, who were
themselves busy trying to attain political and social control within mainstream society and their own institutions.

They used the Bible to attain this control. When dominant society
used the Pauline scripture that asserts that women are to be submissive

---

10. See George Marsden, "Everyone One's Own Interpreter: The Bible, Science,
and Authority in Mid-Nineteenth-Century America"; Vincent L. Wimbush, "Biblical Historical Study as Liberation: Toward an Afro-Christian Hermeneutic," 140;
Monroe Fordham, *Major Themes in Northern Black Religious Thought, 1800–
1860,* 5.

and "silent" in church and society, Julia Foote offered another perspective. Foote maintains that women should not be "kept in bondage by those who say, 'we suffer not a woman to teach,' thus quoting Paul's words but not rightly applying them" (*Experience*, 113). She critiques this scripture-based gender restriction by calling attention to a very important point about historical contextualization. She recognizes that one should not divorce the meaning of an idea or act from the historical or sociological context in which it was created. Nineteenth-century interpreters, to her, are therefore "not rightly using [the Scriptures]." Prescribed guidelines for female roles and behavior in Pauline times were not necessarily applicable to "modern" times. Women were in very different positions in the nineteenth century than they were in Pauline times, and to expect them to live according to expectations of another historical period seemed unrealistic to many black women preachers. Foote strongly suggests that the Bible does not mandate that women be silent, but rather that nineteenth-century society interpreted the Bible this way in an effort to keep women in "bondage." It becomes necessary and important, in Foote's view, to dismiss or ignore these constructs or opinions. Recognizing such negative readings of women's positions as man's own view, man's own opinion, Foote asserts that "Man's opinion weighed nothing to me" (*Experience,* 78).

Emphasizing that nineteenth-century biblical interpreters recognized the impact of their own historical situatedness when reading the Bible was just one hermeneutical approach that black women preachers took to attain space for themselves to preach in this context. An even more profound attack on hegemonic biblical interpretations can be found in their use of what I am calling *typological (gyn)esis.* By this term, I mean that they refer to the Bible for visible woman figures to establish a "genesis," or beginning point, that locates the role of women as either preachers or active participants in ministries. I am drawing from Werner Sollors's concept of "typological ethnogenesis," which he uses to describe the reference by oppressed groups to certain ethnic groups in the Bible in order to find a point of relation or identification.[11] Exemplifying this notion are blacks who identify with the Israelites in the Bible as a way to understand themselves as God's chosen people who

11. Werner Sollors, *Beyond Ethnicity: Consent and Descent in American Culture,* 50.

will make it to a promised land void of racial oppression. With the term *typological (gyn)esis,* I attempt to establish a similar dialectic in regard to women, but it extends beyond the Bible to religious history. These women preachers locate in religious and biblical histories roles that women played in order to account for what was sexist exclusion of women as active agents in religion and the Bible. They used typological (gyn)esis in order to establish a biblical locus from which to refute contemporary gender restrictions that had the potential to undermine their call to preach from the Bible.[12]

Joel 2:28–29 is the scripture most consistently used by black women preachers to establish an exemplary locus in divine will for the right of women to preach: "After this I shall pour out my spirit on all mankind; / your sons and your daughters will prophesy." Appearing repeatedly and consistently in all of the texts by prophesying daughters that I discuss here, this passage is referred to in order to establish gendered space in divine will to refute nineteenth-century gender-restrictive ideologies that suggest otherwise. Reference to this passage is crucial because it indicates a prophecy void of gender bias. By "pouring out [His] spirit upon all flesh," God has already mandated spiritual egalitarianism in terms of who had access to preaching: the "sons and daughters."

Julia Foote provides an excellent example of the typological (gyn)etic use of this passage in a detailed summary of a "mini-sermon" she was called upon to preach to a dying man whom she described as "influential . . . though a sinner" (*Experience,* 104).[13] In this summary, she discusses how in 710 B.C., corn was threshed by oxen who trampled over the corn to separate it from the straw. She indicates that in the nineteenth

---

12. Elizabeth Cady Stanton's *The Woman's Bible* is one of the most extensive typological (gyn)etic projects. In this book, Stanton rewrites the Bible, foregrounding the roles of women and their contributions in biblical history. This was a very bold move for a woman to take in the nineteenth century.

13. This is crucial. It gives an indication of how these women were using typological (gyn)esis not only in their autobiographies but in their sermons as well. Finding and studying these sermons could well result in groundbreaking work. Bettye Collier-Thomas's *Daughters of Thunder* analyzes a few sermons after the 1880s. A project that focused on sermons beyond this time could provide insight into how women in the nineteenth century juxtaposed race- and gender-restrictive ideologies in their interpretations of various scriptures. It could also give insight into how these sermons were presented to audiences that were apparently diverse in terms of sex, age, class, and ethnicity.

century corn was threshed with a flail, as technological advances in a much later historical period had made this process easier. She equates herself with the threshing instrument, sent by God to thresh out sin in these changing historical times. She interestingly subverts this message to indicate divine ordination for women's rights to "thresh," stating: "The passage portrays the Gospel times, though in a more restricted sense it applies to the preachers of the word. Yet in a direct reference to all God's people, who were and are commanded to arise and thresh. Glory to Jesus! now is this prophecy fulfilled—Joel ii.28 and 29. *They* are also commanded to go to God who alone is able to qualify them for their labors by making their horns iron and their hoofs brass" (*Brand,* 104–5). The reference to "all God's people who were and are commanded to arise to thresh" is significant in two ways. First, it embarks upon the notion of divine establishment—God, Himself, has already maintained that "all," regardless of gender, have the right to "thresh," to preach. Society cannot change that. Second, it references this obligatory charge to carry out God's command. It is God's command that whomever he calls to "thresh" must do so in spite of societal restrictions against it.

The reference to the prophecy being fulfilled is also crucial. She establishes not only that women's preaching is divinely ordained, but that her work as a preacher is a realization of the prophecy. This particular sermon offers evidence that God's will for women to preach has been actualized. Finally, the assertion that it is "God who alone is able to qualify them for their labors" levels a profound attack on nineteenth-century society's tendency to use biblical reference to perpetuate the gender myths intended to keep women from the public space of preaching. Foote is also, to use Katie Cannon's term here, "remythologizing divine will." Having qualified women to "thresh," God has indicated that it is His will that they do so. Society is again implicated, for to go against what is divinely ordained is a sin. Society is forced, then, to question its motives for oppressing women by keeping them out of the pulpit. As women preachers, not only must they "thresh" sin out of sinners in the normal sense, but they must also "thresh" out what they see as a societal sin of gender discrimination.

Furthermore, black women preachers employ typological (gyn)esis by establishing women as key role players in Christ's ministry. This is important because the Four Gospels of Matthew, Mark, Luke, and John use stories and teachings to detail Jesus' life on Earth; but since the culture in which they wrote "tended to devalue women and the feminine," such views made their way into their writing. Even though these men shared the views of their culture, the strong feature of the role that women played in Jesus' ministry still managed to come out through the words of Jesus Christ.[14] Stewart closely examines these words to highlight the ways that women helped in the promulgation of Christ's ministry, asking: "Did not . . . Mary Magdalene first declare the resurrection of Christ from the dead? Come said the woman of Samaria, and see a man that told me all things that ever I did, and is not this the Christ" (*Productions*, 75). Stewart reveals that Jesus' actions toward these women reveal not only the significant roles that women play in the spreading and development of his ministry but also the fact that Jesus himself trusted in women's ability to effectively carry out his mission. Mary Magdalene and the woman of Samaria whom Stewart mentions are two favorite examples of this.

MacHaffie's reading of Mary Magdalene as one of Jesus' disciples is especially relevant here. She notes that in the parable of "Jesus the Good Shepherd" in the Gospel of Saint John, John is comparing Jesus' disciples to a sheep that knows his shepherd's voice when the shepherd calls the sheep's name. In this parable, Jesus says: "And when he [the shepherd] brings out his own sheep, he goes before them; and the sheep follow him, for they know his voice" (John 10:11). He then says, "I am the good shepherd. . . . My sheep hear my voice" (John 10:27). Later in the Gospel of John, after Jesus' death and miraculous resurrection, Mary Magdalene is weeping because Jesus' body is not in the tomb in which she had placed him. While she is weeping, Jesus appears to her and "said to her Mary!," and, in keeping with Jesus' description of a disciple, she recognizes the "shepherd's voice." Jesus then instructs Mary to "go to my brethren and say to them, 'I am ascending to My Father, and to My God and your God'" (John 20:16–17). Mary spreads this news. Jesus' resurrection is a major component of the Christian belief, and Mary Magdalene was not only the primary witness to this significant event, but she was key in making it known to the people.

MacHaffie also reads the woman of Samaria as significant to Jesus' ministry, for it is to her that Jesus first reveals that he is the coming

14. MacHaffie, *Her Story: Women in Christian Tradition*, 14, 15.

Messiah. A social outcast because she had five husbands, the woman of Samaria was drawing water from a well when Jesus approached the well and engaged in a conversation with her in which he revealed that he knew that she had five husbands and told her that he was the Messiah whom the Christians believed was coming. "The woman then left her water pot, went to the city," and told the people of her conversation with Jesus. "And many of the Samaritans of that city believed in Him because of the word of the woman who testified." The stories of Mary Magdalene, the woman of Samaria, and others are important because they refute the notion that women in the Bible were silent and subservient. Their stories establish women's roles in biblical history, thus giving women preachers in the nineteenth century precedents from which to claim authority to carry out their obligation to God.

In this regard, black women preachers looked at history in terms of teaching some moral truth, that truth being that women in the nineteenth century had the right to preach. They used another critical approach as well to argue for political change for blacks. They employed a critical biblical approach called *figuralism,* which is defined best by critic Theophus Smith. According to Smith, figuralism is "a hermeneutic or interpretative tradition in which a person or place, object or event, is connected to a second entity in such a way that the first signifies the second and the second fulfills or encompasses the first."[15] In other words, those employing this tradition refer to certain people, places, objects, or events in the Bible that have relevance to their own lives, and they appropriate those things to understand themselves or to change their situation, be it actual change or what Smith calls "pharmacopedic" (mental or spiritual "curing"). Black women preachers use such an approach to argue for political change. Maria Stewart best exemplifies the use of figuralism for racial liberation in the nineteenth century.

One of the largest political issues confronting blacks at the time of Stewart's work was the colonization of free blacks in Liberia. As were David Walker and many of her other contemporaries, Stewart was against colonization to Africa and felt as if many whites' support of this effort provided further evidence of white hypocrisy and racist attitudes in America. She critiques this racist agenda by employing figuralism in

15. Theophus Smith, *Conjuring Culture: The Biblical Formation of Black America,* 70.

the hope of ensuring blacks the right to stay in America and reap the benefits she felt they deserved for the years of hard labor they put into building the nation: "But ah, methinks their hearts are so frozen towards us, they had rather their money should be sunk in the ocean than to administer it to our relief, and I fear, if they dared, like Pharaoh, king of Egypt, they would order every male child among us to be drowned. But the most high God is still able to subdue the lofty pride of these white Americans, as He was the heart of that ancient rebel" (*Productions*, 69). In this case, Stewart is using the figure of Pharaoh to allude to the apocalyptic end awaiting whites in America who continue to deny blacks their freedom. By aligning whites with Pharaoh—whose continual social and economic denial of the Israelites resulted in his army being drowned in the Red Sea—Stewart warns whites of a biblical precedent for the punishment of oppressive behavior, which is the annihilation of the oppressor. In what is clearly what Katie Cannon calls a "remythologizing of divine will" (that is, a rereading of God's intentions), Stewart maintains that the Bible admonishes against such oppressive behavior. Oppressive whites become implicated in the assertion that oppression is a sin for which extermination is the punishment. As Albert Raboteau notes, "America was Egypt, and as long as she continued to enslave and oppress Black Israel, her destiny was in jeopardy. Americans stood under the judgement of God, and unless she repented, the death and destruction visited upon Biblical Egypt would be repeated here."[16]

Stewart further remythologizes divine will in her use of the figural concept of Ethiopianism, employing Psalms 68:31 to implicate oppressive whites as well: "Princes shall come out of Egypt; Ethiopia shall soon stretch out her hands unto God." Cited widely throughout black religious history, some variation of this passage appears in the writings and speeches of nineteenth-century scholars and activists as diverse as Frances E. W. Harper, W. E. B. Du Bois, David Walker, and Alexander Young. It is often referred to and reinterpreted to speak to the experiences of blacks in America, connoting that, as Wilson Moses states, "the rise in the fortunes of Africa and all her scattered children would be accompanied by God's judgment upon the Europeans."[17] Stewart uses

---

16. Albert Raboteau, "African-Americans, Exodus, and the American Israel," 2.

17. Wilson Moses, "The Poetics of Ethiopianism: W.E.B. DuBois and Literary Black Nationalism," 412.

this passage to indicate how class discrimination against blacks in many ways hindered blacks from receiving the "fortunes" from their labor. She states that many "white Americans gained themselves a name" from the hard work and labor of blacks, "while in reality, we have been their principle foundation and support" (*Productions,* 63). Stewart critiques white desire to keep blacks within the confines of domestic and manual labor. She states that "as servants we are respected; but let us presume to aspire higher, our employer regards us no longer" (*Productions,* 54). Using Ethiopianism, Stewart projects that "were it not that the King eternal has declared that Ethiopia shall stretch forth her hands unto God, I should indeed despair" (*Productions,* 54). Stewart invokes divine providence. The Bible indicates that blacks, whom she parallels with the Ethiopians, will experience what Moses calls "a dramatic political, industrial and economic renaissance" in spite of white efforts to oppress them.[18] Were it not divinely mandated, she would "indeed despair."

Finally, the selection of passages that aligns these women preachers with the oppressed in the Bible and that is necessary for figuralism and typological (gyn)esis understandably could be seen as problematic when one considers the fact that these passages came from an androcentric and patriarchal context. Depictions of the oppressed in the Bible are revealed through the perspective of the dominant class. Whites in the nineteenth century probably found no problem reinscribing oppressive tendencies prevalent in the Bible, because as the dominant ruling class their interests in many ways were similar to those of the ruling class in the Bible.

James Mosala, who studies such notions of figuralism as they relate to South Africans, finds this tendency to make connections with situations and circumstances in the world of the Bible somewhat contradictory and self-defeating. He feels that an uncritical acceptance of white theology makes blacks unable to free themselves from whites, and that their reference to the Bible in an effort to attain liberation was an act of further social enslavement. According to Mosala, this act lends itself to a "slavery of hermeneutics." Mosala also asserts that blacks or the oppressed should take into consideration the historical context of biblical stories before connecting to them. In regard to women locating female figures in the Bible to whom they choose to relate, Daphne Hampson feels that appropriating the biblical past is "fraught with difficulty." Hampson asserts

18. Ibid.

that "if what one wishes to find is women who may serve as models . . . I would suggest that the outlook is bleak. This is not surprising when one considers that biblical literature arose in a patriarchal society."[19]

I respond to arguments such as those presented by Hampson and Mosala by aligning my critical goal here with the critical intentions of prophesying daughters in the nineteenth-century context. I am fully aware of the "androcentric," "patriarchal" context in which black women preachers wrote and lived. It is my contention, however, that despite this reality, a close study of their lives provides evidence of alternative ways of not only living but of engaging with and responding to their environment. Their texts require, then, that we understand that despite the fact that the nineteenth century was patriarchal, the texts of black women preachers call for new ways of understanding their context.

Black women preachers took similar critical and theoretical approaches to getting nineteenth-century readers and biblical critics to look for alternative readings of the biblical past. One way that this was most effectively done is found in Jarena Lee's etymological exploration of the word *preach*. Lee argues that those opposed to women preaching in the nineteenth century should consider the fact that the word *preach* may have had different connotations and denotations in biblical times than it does in the nineteenth century. According to Lee, the contemporary (nineteenth-century) use of the word *preach,* which meant "to expound on the scriptures" was inapplicable to biblical times (*Experience,* 12). She felt that "perhaps it was a great deal more simple then" (*Experience,* 12), when the Word of God was basically being spread by word of mouth based on personal testimonies and witnesses. Although some of Jesus' disciples were illiterate, they were still able to preach in the sense that they were instrumental in spreading Jesus' gospel. With this said, Lee points out that women were "preachers" in biblical times. This is why she states that "Mary [Magdalene] did not preach in the 'proper' [meaning current] sense of the term," but that she, being a key witness to the resurrection of Christ and spreading the news, did indeed preach. Lee asks: "Then did not Mary, a woman, preach the gospel? for she preached the resurrection of the crucified God" (*Experience,* 11). Julia Foote's assertion that when "Paul said 'Help these women who labored with me in the

---

19. Itumeleng J. Mosala, *Biblical Hermeneutics and Black Theology in South Africa,* 13; Daphne Hampson, *Theology and Feminism,* 103.

Gospel,' he certainly meant that they did more than pour out tea," speaks to this idea as well (*Brand*, 79). By providing revised notions of proselytizing in regard to biblical history, nineteenth-century black women preachers were able to open up space for themselves to preach.

Although women were expected to act and behave in prescribed ways because (to paraphrase a popular Christian song) "the Bible told them so," black women preachers—trusting the legitimacy of their own interpretative rights to the Bible given them by their conversion experience—believed that the Bible told them something different. Consequently, they found in their own biblical historical contexts sites from which to articulate their identifications of themselves in a social context that otherwise rendered them subjectless.

SIX

Prophetic Works

PROPHESYING DAUGHTERS AND
SOCIAL ACTIVISM—THE CASE OF
FRANCES JOSEPH GAUDET

M ost scholars of black feminist thought pinpoint the late 1800s
and the turn of the century as a defining era in black women's
social and political involvement. Though prior to this moment black
women had always played active roles in shaping and defining black
life and culture, at the turn of the century they were more actively and
vocally questioning the status quo and were quite assertively projecting
their own views on the direction in which not only black Americans but
also American society in general should head. These race women knew
that what black women were doing collectively was consciously correct-
ing what had been up to that point a deliberate effort to exclude them
from the American social picture.[1] It could have been taken as a given
that white male–run institutions were marginalizing them, but they also
faced isolation within their own institutions, such as churches, civic
organizations, and universities. White women created their own organizations and movements without including black women's issues and
concerns either. Such exclusionary practices did not keep many black
women from realizing that if they were going to be taken seriously as
active agents for change, they were going to have to take matters in their
own hands and become politically involved and vocal.

---

1. "Race women" were black women who actively participated in educational,
political, and moral programs for racial uplift.

Paralleling black women's active public involvement, a consciousness emerged that women like Josephine St. Pierre Ruffin, Ida B. Wells-Barnett, Anna Julia Cooper, Hallie Quinn Brown, Mary McLeod Bethune, Fannie Jackson Coppin, and Frances E. W. Harper were not only actively shaping how they were going to be perceived as black women, but also that they had clear agendas for taking responsibility for the direction of the race. They used speeches, novels, essays, articles, and other forms of expression to speak out against the racial and social wrongs that blacks were suffering during the late 1890s: the increase in lynchings, constant attacks by mobs, and the daily indignities that they had to suffer under Jim Crowism. They began to create clubs such as the Women's Era Club (1894), the National Federation of Colored Women (1895), and the National Colored Women's League (1897) to collectively organize their efforts, thus launching what is now commonly known as the black women's club movement. So prevalent was black women's public and social presence that Frances E. W. Harper declared the period she was living in to be the "woman's era."[2]

Because of black women's active public involvement during this time, many scholars such as Frances Smith Foster, Hazel Carby, Patricia Hill Collins, Carla Peterson, Deborah McDowell, and Paula Giddings rightfully recognize this period as a critical moment in the development of black feminist thought. While contemporary discussions of these race women have provided invaluable insight into the role of black women in shaping social consciousness, they have somewhat slighted the roles that prophesying daughters played in social development. A lot of this has to do with the limited attention scholars have given religion, although scholars have indeed discussed the importance of morality and virtue to race women at the turn of the century. Issues like having high moral values and displaying virtue at all times were at the forefront of the nineteenth-century black feminist platform. Black women realized that they "were seen as immoral scourges," and that "the idea of a moral Black woman was incredible." Consequently, "black women have created and cultivated a set of ethical values that allow them to prevail against the

---

2. Harper termed this time period the "woman's era" while giving a speech as one of six black women invited to the primarily white World's Congress of Representative Women in May 1893.

odds, with moral integrity, in their ongoing participation in the white-male-capitalist value system."[3]

The scholarly discussions of prophesying daughters have tended to center around the moral issues, inspired, perhaps, by the fact that women preachers and religious activists such as Maria Stewart declared that they "possess[ed] nothing but moral capability" (*Productions*, 52). Others felt that their careers as preachers were centered around shaping the "mental and moral culture" of blacks and Americans (*Experience*, 29). Because of this prevailing focus on morality and virtue, the few discussions of black women preachers present them as being concerned primarily with religious and spiritual matters, leaving little space to consider them as the very active agents for social change that they actually were. Black women preachers are generally not viewed as using their professional careers—which are grounded in religion—to change social conditions in ways similar to those in which Ida B. Wells used her journalism and Frances E. W. Harper used her literature.

Evelyn Higginbotham has demonstrated the political roles that women played within the Baptist institution. She focuses primarily on what women congregation members were doing within this movement to bring about social and political changes. Her study is extremely important in that it challenges the notion that women were not actively involved in bringing about social change within their religious institutions. However, her study omits serious discussion of women like Jarena Lee, Julia Foote, and other prophesying daughters who felt called both to preach and to change society. In fact, Higginbotham states that "focus on the ministry fails to capture adequately the gender dimension of the church's racial mission." This view does not factor in how prophesying daughters challenged the very institutional structure of churches by positioning themselves to shape and influence views and by taking on the serious responsibility of saving souls, acts usually reserved for men. Many of these prophesying daughters, as Bettye Collier-Thomas has pointed out, "travelled extensively, speaking to thousands of women (and men) who came out to support their ministries and to hear their powerful messages."[4] These messages—as the sermons Collier-Thomas

3. Paula Giddings, *When and Where I Enter: The Impact of Black Women on Race and Sex in America*, 82; Katie Cannon, *Black Womanist Ethics*, 75.

4. Higginbotham, *Righteous Discontent*; Collier-Thomas, *Daughters of Thunder*, 283,

includes in her book reveal—contain philosophies put forth by prophesying daughters on how society can be changed through moral and religious conversions.

Other scholars who have done research on prophesying daughters individually or collectively have also somewhat downplayed their roles as social activists. William Andrews, Joanne Braxton, Jualyne Dodson, and Cheryl Townsend-Gilkes, for example, do indeed recognize that social ideologies of racism, sexism, and classism affected these women's careers, but they do not necessarily consider the reverse—how these women used their careers to effect change in the social arena.

Braxton, for example, believes that these women used religion as a mechanism for their individual and personal improvement. She does acknowledge that these women desired community development, but she does not examine how they tried to achieve it. Braxton states that the texts of black women preachers and missionaries reveal primarily "their quest for personal power" as well as their "quest for spiritual perfection in an imperfect world." In regard to social activism, Braxton mentions the desires of these women to change things and shows that some of their interrogations of social constraints affecting their lives were put forth in order to spiritually strengthen themselves as individuals. Consequently, she concludes that narratives "by Black women preachers focus almost wholly on spiritual matters and show less concern with temporal issues except as they relate directly to spiritual development."[5]

William Andrews takes a similar stance. In his discussion of the social import of the autobiographies of three black women preachers, he does acknowledge that their texts speak "to the question of the social significance of the careers of Black women activists on the religious front in nineteenth-century America." However, Andrews holds that from a social perspective, the central concern of these texts "is the growth of authentic, individually authorized selfhood." Andrews privileges the individual religious subject and discusses the ways in which social ideals infringed upon this "individually authorized selfhood." Such a depiction of these women implies that their interactions with such social infringements as racism and sexism resulted primarily from their strong effort to preserve their newly acquired selfhood. Protecting their God-inspired, newly converted identity was indeed extremely important to

5. Braxton, *Black Women Writing Autobiography,* 49, 55.

them, and it was a necessity if they were to be successful at carrying out God's command to spread His Word. However, to assert that their reasons for attacking social mores were motivated primarily by self-preservation does not allow much space for a consideration of the often "selfless" roles they played in overall societal preservation and racial uplift. Andrews writes—in a conclusion similar to Braxton's—that "none of these women thought of herself as a social visionary or reformer of social institutions; none put forward any utopian schemes for new communities, Christian or otherwise."[6]

Jualyne Dodson also provides excellent insight into the significance of black women's presence in the A.M.E. Church in the nineteenth century. In fact, Dodson makes known many other preachers besides those discussed in this study, thereby demonstrating that there was indeed a large community of black women who were preaching and traveling all over the country to do so. Dodson's article has even further significance. Besides providing a context that speaks to a black female preaching presence in the nineteenth century, it locates a space for black women in the beginning phases of black church development. However, she limits her contextualization of black women preacher's ecclesiastical struggles to a particular denomination's movements. Consequently, she does not make any larger correlations or parallels between their internal struggles against exclusion on the basis of gender and larger issues of gender and race. One might speculate that this oversight was caused by Dodson's focusing specifically on A.M.E. Church records, polities, and histories as the basis for her argument, but among the documents she considers is the autobiography of Jarena Lee. In fact, she uses excerpts from Lee's autobiography and makes lengthy commentary on how Lee's narrative reflects her specific struggle within the church. Dodson concludes—based on her reading of Lee's autobiography and the many other records she uses—that these women's challenges to patriarchal or exclusionary structures and tendencies were strictly church specific.

In fact, Dodson makes the assertion that "these women were not revolutionaries bent on shaking structures, but reformers within a more inclusive and just organization." Taking a stance similar to those of An-

---

6. Andrews, *Sisters of the Spirit*, 16, 20.

drews and Braxton, Dodson also asserts that it was for individual preservation and not a larger communal one that black women preachers attacked sexist and racist ideologies. For example, in regard to clear distinctions of gender roles and rules in the black church, Dodson does not associate black women's fight to correct internal gender problems with larger feminist arguments of equality. She states that "not feminist claims for the rights of all women, but their sense of their own special call led them to challenge male domination in the church." Neither does she make the larger connection between these women's fight against racism in the black church as an institution and their fight against racism itself as an institution. Dodson states that "in most instances, preaching women were extremely committed to protesting white racism in the tradition of African Methodism, but they had no broader social program."[7]

To these discussions of black women preachers and social involvement, I add a wider reading of their texts, which analyzes ways in which their views of themselves as prophesying daughters translated into their effecting social change. I accept Hazel Carby's assertion that the writing of African American women should not be looked at "within a social or literary history as merely a context for analysis." Instead, it is necessary to look at their works "not only as determined by the social conditions within which they were produced, but as cultural artifacts that shape the social condition they enter."[8] Therefore, I assert that, while the depictions of prophesying daughters as moral and spiritual are accurate, these black women preachers were also socially conscious and aware, and that their texts are indeed "artifacts" that shaped the social conditions during the times in which they were written. Their texts are religious, but they emphasize religion as a primary factor for racial and social uplift. The autobiographies are not necessarily about the subjects themselves but are rather about women in relation to how they promote political and social change through religious conviction.

In order to provide a broader description of black feminist social involvement that includes black women preachers and religious women, I examine in this chapter the narratives that range from the beginning of the nineteenth century to the turn of the twentieth century. I use the

7. Dodson, "Nineteenth-Century A.M.E. Preaching Women," 277–78.
8. Hazel Carby, *Reconstructing Womanhood*, 95.

specific example of the autobiography of Frances Joseph Gaudet to further depict the ways in which prophesying daughters appropriated the religious to critique and change the secular. Gaudet published her text in 1913 and used religious and moral principles that were the basis of her perception of herself as a prophesying daughter to address the same social issues of concern to many of her female activist contemporaries. My specific focus here upon black women preachers who were members of or closely affiliated with the A.M.E. Church is not intended to exclude women preachers of other denominations. The work of the prophesying daughters I discuss here provides ground for understanding the overall impact in the nineteenth century of active preaching women of other denominations as well.

As I discussed in chapter one, there are several reasons for the absence of critical space to consider black women preachers as social activists: (1) the tendency in the academy to privilege the secular and the scientific; (2) institutional exclusions from their records of the prevalent and active roles women preachers and members played in the churches; and (3) white religious feminists' marginalization of black women preachers from their social movements. Scholars such as Collier-Thomas, Dodson, Townsend-Gilkes, and Andrews have at least made it known that a black female preaching presence did exist in the nineteenth century. And, thanks to the efforts by the Schomburg Library of Nineteenth-Century Black Women Writers, we now have access to a volume of texts by some of these women preachers (Jarena Lee, Julie Foote, Maria Stewart, and Virginia Broughton).

Frances Smith Foster provides one of the first attempts to move away from viewing black women preacher's texts in a strictly theological, spiritual context. She devotes an entire chapter to the ways in which Jarena Lee's religious experiences, life, and journal contribute to a black female literary tradition. Foster states that "understanding Jarena Lee's narrative in particular and African American women's writings in general requires that one understands how their texts reconstruct both traditions in ways that resemble both but are unique in themselves."[9]Foster recognizes the uniqueness that Lee's religious conviction adds to her texts, but placing her text within this tradition of African American women's

9. Foster, *Written By Herself,* 59

writing invites viewing Lee's text and others similar to hers within or out of the context of all the factors that characterized black women writing in the nineteenth century. One of the main characteristics of this tradition, for example, was the very overt attack the authors made on various social issues concerning race and gender. For instance, Harriet Jacobs's *Incidents in the Life of a Slave Girl* details the dilemma she faced in trying to assert her own notions of womanhood in a social context that did not include black women in the category of "women." Frances Harper's poems, short stories, and novels all speak out against racism and sexism and for temperance and suffrage. Harriet E. Wilson's *Our Nig: or, Ketches from the Life of a Free Black, In a Two-Story White House, North. Showing that Slavery's Shadows Fall Even There* exposes the new form of poverty, racism, and sexism that slavery took on in the North in the lives of "free" blacks. Many other literary works by black women addressed and challenged social mores of the day, and Lee and other black women preachers were part of this tradition. Their religious convictions and their moral and spiritual standings did not cancel out their propensity to be active agents for social change. I make this assertion not to ask for a separate look at them but to include them in the overall context of black women who were actively taking charge of shaping attitudes toward race in nineteenth-century society.

Situating the autobiographies by women preachers within the literary context laid out by Foster, one can see their significance as testimonies of their active presence in social movements. A historical overview of the texts of Jarena Lee, Julia Foote, Maria Stewart, and Frances Joseph Gaudet shows an evolution of the political significance of the autobiographies of prophesying daughters from the antebellum period to the postbellum period to the turn of the century. The time span covered in these texts ranges from around 1783 (when Jarena Lee was born) until 1913 (when Gaudet's text was published). During this period of over one hundred years—through slavery, emancipation, Reconstruction, and Post-Reconstruction—the texts of black women preachers reflect an evolution of their political presence within each of these historical moments in which they were active in their careers. They also show ways in which these particular moments affected the approach that they took to writing their autobiographies.

For example, Jarena Lee and Maria Stewart were socially active antebellum prophesying daughters. Along with slavery, the social issues that most affected blacks were emigration, colonization, and assimilation. Blacks also had to contend with two extremely common arguments often used to justify their political and social conditions: the questioning of their humanity and the overall assertion that they did not have souls. Lee's and Stewart's texts show that they saw the political connection between these views and the exploitation of blacks. They used their texts to consciously refute such notions in order to establish the existence of a real black spiritual subject.

William Andrews notes that as spiritual autobiographers writing during the pre-emancipation period, Lee and Stewart "had to lay the necessary intellectual groundwork by proving that Black people were as much chosen by God for eternal salvation as whites." Their works were a "reclamation of the Afro-American's spiritual birthright."[10] A clear example of how the notion that blacks had no souls affected the treatment of prophesying daughters is seen in Lee's account of a confrontation she has with a white man she describes as "A Deist . . . who said that he did not believe the coloured people had any souls" (*Experience*, 19). She states further that, in fact, "he was sure that they had none" (*Experience*, 19). Lee recounts that once when she was preaching, this man showed up "with others who came from curiosity to hear the woman preacher" and to see if she really was capable of an act that only those with souls and intelligence could perform (*Experience*, 19). Despite the fact that throughout her sermon this man, who took a seat next to where she was standing, "boldly tried to look [her] out of countenance," Lee continued to preach. After her sermon, Lee notes, this man admitted to other people that "he believed I had the worth of souls at heart" (*Experience*, 19). To this statement, Lee responded that "this language was different from what it was a little time before, as he now seemed to admit that coloured people had souls, as it was to these I was chiefly speaking" (*Experience*, 19). Lee also notes that this man, who "was a great slave holder, and had been very cruel," changed his treatment of slaves after hearing her sermon: "it was said of him that he became greatly altered in his ways for the better" (*Experience*, 19).

Why, as the writer of her own narrative, did Lee feel it necessary to write about this man's incredulity at and distrust of the possibility that

10. Andrews, *To Tell a Free Story*, 8.

she could possess a soul and her ability to convert the souls of blacks? Why was it even more important that she showed her propensity to evoke change in him? She wrote about his changed behavior in order to identify the philosophical and political basis for his former behavior. Philosophically, his views represent the existence of the heathen/nonheathen binary that served to justify his maltreatment of his slaves. If they had no souls, then they were not humans, and nonhumans did not deserve, in this view, humane treatment. Obviously, Lee's sermon offered evidence to the contrary, showing that blacks did indeed have souls. Politically, of course, his adhering to and promoting this social binary maintained his power over the slaves. It even informed his failed attempt to intimidate Lee into submission and admission of the legitimacy of his views. Of course, Lee interpreted his actions as an opportunity to apply her own philosophical understanding of herself as a prophesying daughter, using her mandate by God to enact social change. That he basically admitted that blacks did have souls and then treated his slaves differently as a result of her sermon is evidence of her ability to create change. Although this change was not far-reaching, it at least benefited the slaves of this man. Furthermore, by writing about this man's skepticism and his subsequent change in her text, Lee is proselytizing in the hope of establishing in the minds of any doubtful readers the belief that blacks do have souls, and that she, a black woman, can change white and black souls.

Using the text to provide evidence that blacks do have souls, both Lee and Maria Stewart go even further to foreground in their texts the conception and birth of their spirituality and the various avenues through which their souls were manifested. As indicated in chapter three, detailing their conversion experience—which chronicles their growth into spiritual being—was a strategy employed to critique the social restrictions encoded in denying blacks' spiritual rights. Lee and Stewart indicate that the issue is not that blacks did not have souls; rather, it is the existence of social guidelines stipulating or suggesting otherwise. As a result, Lee and Stewart emphasized repeatedly the existence of their souls. Lee made constant reference to her ability to convert souls as testimony to her having one herself. She states, for example: "I am fully persuaded that the Lord called me to labor according to what I have received, in his vineyard. If he has not, how could he consistently bear testimony in favor of my poor labors, in awakening and converting sinners?" (*Experience*, 12).

A more profound critique of this notion is seen in the format Stewart chooses for her text. Unlike Lee, Stewart provides several meditations followed by prayers in the text. These meditations and prayers are intended to show her dialogue with God, and they reveal her thoughts and concerns about moral and religious philosophies, as well as the impact that political issues have on morality. Providing her meditations and prayers serves two significant strategic purposes. First, the meditations and prayers show her ability to think logically and to analyze religious concerns. This in turn proves that she is spiritual and therefore does indeed have a soul. Second, in almost all of the fourteen meditations that she provides, she makes clear and direct reference to her soul. Doing so strategically insists on its existence. For example, she emphasizes that "soon after I presented myself before the Lord in the holy ordinance of baptism, my soul become filled with holy meditations and sublime ideas; and my ardent wish and desire have ever been, that I might become a instrument in the hands of God, winning some poor souls to Christ" (*Productions*, 23–24).

As does Lee, Stewart also critiques the impact that racial prejudice and the exploitation of black labor has on stagnating the souls of black folk. She states: "O, horrible idea, indeed! To possess noble souls aspiring after high and honorable acquirements, yet confined by the chains of ignorance and poverty to lives of continual drudgery and toil" (*Productions*, 53). She states further that "continual hard labor deadens the energies of the soul, and benumbs the faculties of the mind; the ideas become confined, the mind barren, and like the scorching sands of Arabia, produces nothing" (*Productions*, 53–54). Contrary to popular nineteenth-century ideology, Stewart's views presuppose the existence of souls in black people. Her critique instead focuses on the societal conditions that prevent souls from developing to their full potential. Lee and Stewart viewed their arguments asserting the existence of black people's souls as a political strategy contributing to the uplift of the black race. Providing evidence of the spiritual worth of blacks would lead to better treatment of blacks as a whole and would open the space for political and social improvement.

In the second half of the nineteenth century, when blacks' attention and energies were channeled in a sociopolitical direction and focused on defining black identity, a change occurred in the way in which prophesying was used. The texts published during this period are more assertive in tone than were Lee's and Stewart's texts, which were published in 1849 and 1835, respectively.[11] There is less emphasis on proving the presence of the soul; the focus seems to shift to an active confrontation of issues such as lynching, capital punishment, Jim Crowism, and temperance. Julia Foote's autobiography, *A Brand Plucked from the Fire*, represents how prophesying is employed during this period.

Foote was born in 1823 and converted at age fifteen, and her text was published in 1886. This means that a large part of her religious life extended across the historical periods of slavery, emancipation, and Reconstruction. Her transhistorical situation provides invaluable insight into both how prophesying evolved and how the prophesying daughters defined their roles in response to the social changes during these periods. To women who felt called to preach at the time she was publishing her text, Foote says, "[Y]ou may think you have hard times, but let me tell you, I feel that the lion and the lamb are lying down together as compared to the state of things 25 to 30 years ago" (*Brand,* 89). Written around 1886 and referring to the antebellum period when women's roles were even more strictly defined, this statement provides insight into the immobility encoded in gender guidelines in the nineteenth century. The "hard times" that Foote's contemporaries were enduring were a direct result of opposition to women preaching. Foote's comparison of the sexism that existed around 1886 with that from "25 or 30 years ago" speaks also to a continued history of sexism toward women preachers. It suggests as well some progress in the movement against the effort to keep women out of the pulpit.

Foote's preaching across two historical periods also allows for an understanding of how women preachers adjusted their prophesying to deal with the social conditions confronting them. On one occasion, Foote was preaching in Baltimore when a slave master in search of a runaway forced himself into a boardinghouse she was in. Despite such immediate physical dangers and the possibility of being enslaved themselves, Foote and other women preachers continued to travel all over the country. As prophesying daughters, she and her fellow women preachers dared to

---

11. An earlier version of Lee's text was published in 1836.

continue to travel and to minister because they felt strong enough in their convictions to endure threats to their own well-being if such fortitude meant enacting social change.

Writing in 1886, Foote states: "thank the dear Lord we do not have to suffer such indignities now" (*Brand,* 99). However, she still acknowledges that many of the injustices inherent in the system of slavery were still present in its aftermath: "The monster, Slavery, is not yet dead in all its forms" (*Brand,* 99). Seeing herself as someone called by God to effect social change, Foote refused to acquiesce to any of the new forms of slavery. On one occasion, she declined an invitation from a white Methodist church that wanted her to speak but would not allow blacks to attend the services: "I would not agree to any such arrangements, and, therefore, I did not speak for them" (Brand, 99). This refusal shows a consciousness of and unwillingness to participate in socially embedded racial injustice. The contradiction inherent in an invitation that was apparently a validation of her as a Christian but also a rejection of her race was an insult to this consciousness. Her refusal to accept such hypocrisy shows how she used prophesying as a challenge to racial degradation.

When Frances Joseph Gaudet was writing at the turn of the century, blacks were becoming increasingly established both economically and politically. Black women made substantial contributions to this development. They actively participated in the temperance and suffrage movements, and they held professional positions and jobs as doctors, lawyers, and teachers. Black women preachers were at the forefront of racial progress as well, establishing and helping build schools, orphanages, and nursing homes and traveling to speak out against racism, sexism, and other forms of discrimination. Spiritual autobiographies of black women preachers and missionaries during this time reflect a security in their role as shapers of black destiny. They employed religion not only to inspire black progress but also to challenge institutions and ideologies that were impeding black growth. The spiritual narratives of turn-of-the-century writers such as Frances Joseph Gaudet and Virginia Broughton (1907) still employ some of the basic elements of the antebellum and postbellum spiritual autobiographies. Their texts contain a version of their conversion experiences in the early pages. The travel motif is prevalent as well. The Bible is also appropriated for social and personal liberation. In their spiritual autobiographies, however, these later writers exhibit a more assertive, politically charged religiosity that reflects another phase in the evolution of the role of spirituality and religion in black female sociopolitical life.

Frances Joseph Gaudet fairly represents these preaching social activists. Gaudet was a preacher, prison reformer, criminologist, legal assistant, and writer, and she figures in this authoritative phase of black female spiritual autobiography by using her text as a political weapon, primarily by showing the significance of religion to black advancement. Her involvement in various organizations and her work with prison reform, temperance, and juvenile delinquency, along with her Washingtonian approach to education, won her local, national, and international acclaim. Her autobiography details her individual accomplishments in these areas while simultaneously situating her within the context of black women who were active in trying to attain cultural and historical influence. These black women preachers took political, sexual, and personal responsibility for themselves, and they participated actively in racial uplift. Prophesying daughters like Gaudet had a very strong presence in these social and political arenas, assertively projecting their own ideas and solutions for racial progress and institutionalizing many programs or "remedies" that were grounded in religion.

According to one of the letters of attestation that prefaced her 1913 autobiography, Gaudet was "the first American woman to do mission work among Negro prisoners" (*Leadeth*, 2). As a preacher, Gaudet had as her primary agenda prison reform and the education and protection of abandoned and orphaned black children. She felt as if her call to preach directed her specifically to prisoners. She lived in Louisiana during the time when poor treatment of blacks in prison and the exploitative use of black prison labor through the convict leasing system were prevalent. This convict leasing system proved quite profitable for many southern planters who were left in a quandary in the aftermath of slavery. As a result, many blacks were wrongly accused of crimes and sent to prison to be leased out as free labor to local farmers. Angela Davis notes that through such a system, "[b]lack people were forced to play the same old roles carved out for them by slavery. Men and women alike were arrested and imprisoned at the slightest pretext—in order to be leased out by the authorities as convict laborers." She states further that "this perversion of the criminal justice system was oppressive to the ex-slave population as a whole."[12]

Gaudet speaks out strongly against a criminal justice system that served to wrongfully oppress and enslave blacks. She fought to ensure that "every state in the Union would abolish the leasing of its convicts to contractors" (*Leadeth*, 50). She saw it as dehumanizing and demoralizing and felt as if "[n]o more diabolical plan was ever hatched to punish the erring citizen" (*Leadeth*, 50), adding that "the contractor works the prisoners early and late with no food, bad sleeping quarters, the consequence being a high death rate. Very little, if any, reformatory measures are used" (*Leadeth*, 50). The convict lease system was of such financial value to the southern agricultural economy that Gaudet concludes, based on detailed research and statistics, that "the Negro convict [was] more essential to the State than the Negro educator" (*Leadeth*, 54).

In addition to revealing the exploitative nature of convict leasing, Gaudet's prison reform work also revealed other forms of discriminatory and cruel treatment of black and other prisoners. She notes that women were often raped, since "the men had charge of the keys that locked the doors to the women's cells" (*Leadeth*, 40). In detailing the poor conditions of the prisoners, she notes that many times "parish officials did not furnish clothes for them" (*Leadeth*, 18). Gaudet was especially opposed to the imprisonment of children, revealing that "little boys of all sizes were placed in the yard with men who had committed almost every crime on the calendar" (*Leadeth*, 18). Finally, she was also concerned about the children of many of the prisoners, many of whom she felt were "thrown upon the mercies of a cruel world" (*Leadeth*, 28).

Gaudet set out to remedy the problems produced by the prison system, which she felt destroyed the moral capabilities of the prisoners and society. Concerned with the state of prisoners' spiritual and moral standing, Gaudet felt that "innocent or guilty, I feel that God wants us to reach even the prison bound to tell them of His wondrous love" (*Leadeth*, 21). She saw her work as a prison reformer as a tool for moral and social reform, noting that "during the eight years of my prison work, over five hundred souls were converted to Christ. . . . Eleven hundred more pledged themselves to lead better lives" (*Leadeth*, 17). Whether the prisoners converted

12. Angela Davis, *Women, Race, and Class,* 89.

to Christianity or not, Gaudet still unrelentingly fought for the rights of prisoners and for better prison conditions. She wrote letters for the prisoners, secured clothing by "becoming a beggar," and preached to the prisoners, providing moral and mental support (*Leadeth*, 39). She assisted lawyers in obtaining the information needed to free the falsely accused, and in cases where lawyers refused to help, she acquired the information and presented it in court herself.

One example of her frequent role as a legal researcher and public defender was in a case in which a young man who was visiting New Orleans had been falsely accused of pickpocketing, along with two other men. He convinced Gaudet that he was innocent, explaining that he had been in the wrong place at the wrong time. After a lawyer refused the case, Gaudet went over to the court and asked to see the papers of commitment (*Leadeth*, 29). Gaudet writes that upon reading these papers,

> I was not satisfied. I said to myself, "I believe my boy not guilty. . . ."
> I made up my mind to get all the favorable evidence I could from his
> town. . . . Having secured this, I took letters when his trial came up and
> went as a witness on the stand, proved he had a good character, was never
> in prison before and was simply a victim of circumstances. . . . The case
> was given to a jury, they went out about an hour when they filed into
> court, rendered a verdict of guilty for two; but my boy was liberated.
> (*Leadeth*, 29–30)

This story demonstrates Gaudet's concern for the prisoners, as well as her sense of authority, her confidence, her ability to secure the proper evidence to free "[her] boy," and her willingness to utilize this confidence in court.

Later Gaudet expanded her volunteer work beyond the prisons to aid young people who were left homeless when their parent(s) were imprisoned or when their parents abandoned them. She became aware that several prisons incarcerated young boys to keep them off the street. She vowed "to bring about a better condition of affairs to save these helpless children" (*Leadeth*, 118). She began keeping as many children as possible at her home, teaching them self-help skills and moral values. When she realized that her home was too small to house a growing number of children, she began to solicit funds to build a home for them. With financial assistance from philanthropists such as Ida A. Richardson and Albert Baldwin, and through the labor and hard work of Sarah Wagner, a "Mrs. B.," and others, Gaudet was able to found the Colored Industrial Home for Boys and Girls in 1902.

The Industrial Home focused on giving children vocational and agricultural training and teaching them moral and religious values. They were instructed in farming, cooking, sewing, and carpentry as well as general business skills. As Violet H. Bryan states, Gaudet "based [the school's] program very much on the Booker T. Washington model."[13] Gaudet was aware of Washington's approach to founding Tuskegee Institute: "I have the picture of Tuskegee's great industrial institute in mind and I look back to see whence it came. I see Booker T. Washington coming through hard trials and many cares, coming to take his place and to lead his people out of the wilderness of ignorance. Tuskegee, thou art as a hill whose rays are reflected throughout the universe. May the sunshine of thy glory continue to dawn on benighted Africa" (*Leadeth*, 101). This adulatory tribute to Tuskegee appears in her text after Gaudet digresses from providing information on the Industrial Home to ponder the present and potential future conditions of the Negro. She felt that the Negro would be among the greatest races of the world, largely due to institutions like hers and Washington's that emphasized a construction of black identity in which economic success was grounded in industrial and agricultural skills. Gaudet was certainly aware of other education-based alternatives being proposed during this Post-Reconstruction era to better the conditions of blacks: "Of course, I am fully aware of the educational needs of our race. We need educated men and women" (*Leadeth*, 102). However, since financial troubles had prevented her from receiving a college degree, Gaudet knew that higher education was not accessible

---

13. Violet H. Bryan, "Frances Joseph Gaudet: Black Philanthropist," 47. Bryan provides a history of the Gaudet School. In poor health, Gaudet decided in 1919 to offer the school to the Diocese of the Episcopal Church because she wanted long-lasting sponsorship for the school. At the 1921 convention, the offer was officially accepted. Gaudet continued to serve as the principal until she resigned because of poor eyesight. In 1943, the school had 240 students, mostly of high school age. In 1949, the diocese decided to make Gaudet an "AA" college preparatory high school. Because of subsequent poor enrollment, the diocese in 1952 sold ninety-two acres of the Gaudet land to the Orleans Parish School Board to build a high school for blacks. For the 1954–1955 school year, the school was closed. In 1955, however, the diocese opened Gaudet Episcopal Home, carrying on Gaudet's purpose by taking in homeless and orphaned black boys and girls between the ages of four and sixteen. Today Episcopal Community Services has a Gaudet Fund that sponsors several programs.

for all blacks: "[B]ut for that class that can not attain higher education, let us give them what we can. But by all means, let us emphasize industrial education and training. Let us teach the rising generations that life is only worth living when we work, work, work and keep on working" (*Leadeth,* 139).

Gaudet lived by this creed of "work." In her work for the Industrial School and within the prison, legal, and juvenile systems, she was brave, ambitious, talented, and determined. She felt obligated to help better the conditions of the black race despite the adversities of classism, racism, and sexism. She applied her concern for her race and for society at large to institute change. What she could not do locally and single-handedly, she did by joining local, national, and international organizations and clubs that shared her own goals. Gaudet epitomized the black woman at the forefront of the "woman's era."

Although she emphasized religion as an agent for social change—a factor distinguishing her from many of contemporary black women social activists—as an activist, Gaudet experienced some of the same problems with marginalization and exclusion from mainstream politics as did her contemporaries. In making their decisions concerning the plight of blacks and whites in America, white men certainly did not consult black (or white) women. Black men often excluded black women from their movements for racial uplift. Many white women—who themselves were oppressed under this same patriarchal system—excluded black women from their movements and organizations on the basis of race, even though their objectives and concerns were often the same.

For example, the Frances E. Willard Christian Temperance Union was formed during the temperance movement, which "was largely the creation of middle-class white women who directed their energies toward reforming the lower classes, whom they often saw as the true abusers placing yet another burden on society."[14] Proponents of the temperance movement saw alcohol as a destroyer of homes and morals, a position that appealed to Gaudet and her black female contemporaries, who "in 1895–1925 emphasized developing and strengthening the home" (*Leadeth,* 206). Unfortunately for black women, many of the white national and state temperance organizations denied them membership. Another

---

14. Cynthia Neverdon-Morton, *Afro-American Women of the South and the Advancement of the Race, 1895–1925,* 206.

example of the role that racial segregation played in reform efforts is shown by the white General Federation of Women's Clubs denying black women admission to their national convention in 1889. Black women were also denied full participation in the Columbian Exposition in Chicago in 1893, which was considered one of the biggest arenas for social and political exchange and was intended to display the accomplishments of Americans. Paula Giddings has noted that although "Afro-Americans as a group were not allowed to participate," a few black women were selected. But, according to Giddings, "they were well aware of the true reasons for that exclusion."[15]

Not letting rejection hinder their obligation to uplift the black race, black women began to form their own organizations, such as the Women's Era Club (1894), the National Colored Women's League (1897), and the National Federation of Colored Women (1895)—these latter two organizations later merged to form the National Association of Colored Women Clubs of America—to carry out their goals. Although, as Hazel Carby argues, black women's struggle "to achieve adequate representation within the women's suffrage and temperance movements had been continually undermined by a pernicious and persistent racism," few black women were to be eventually admitted to some of these organizations.[16] However, their struggle continued after admission because they then were in a position where they had to prove themselves.

Like many of her black female contemporaries, Gaudet faced rejection from various organizations, but she persevered, eventually becoming the president of the Christian Temperance Union of Louisiana and the superintendent of the Prison Reform Association. As one of the few black female officeholders in these organizations and as the first black person daring to do prison reform for blacks, Gaudet encountered the predicament of otherness that manifested itself in an exoticization of her person and work. Describing her trip to Edinburgh, Scotland, as a delegate to the International World's Women's Christian Temperance Union Convention in 1900, Gaudet states: "My two friends, Miss Lynch and Mrs. Lawson, came in and we were the only persons of color in that large assembly. It seemed as if everyone was looking at us" (*Leadeth*, 62). Gaudet again indicated self-consciousness of her racial difference

15. Giddings, *When and Where I Enter*, 86.
16. Carby, *Reconstructing Womanhood*, 4.

when describing a voyage to Belfast: "I was the only brown person on board, and everyone seemed to eye me with a 'I wonder-if-her-color-will-wash-out' expression on their faces" (*Leadeth*, 85). Despite the attention Gaudet's difference attracted, she still presented well-received speeches and continued traveling to make contacts to secure funds for her Industrial Home and for her prison reform work.

As the first black woman to do prison reform work, Gaudet inspired some observers to compare her accomplishments and talents with those of white female reformers. One of the letters of attestation prefacing Gaudet's text states:

> As beautiful Elizabeth Fry, the Angel of Newgate and many other prisons, and next to Howard, the greatest of prison reformers, labored among criminals of her time, Frances A. Joseph, a women of the Negro race, is laboring among prisoners, Black and white, in Southern jails. That Elizabeth Fry, wealthy and of the highest social position should impress people of station and authority, overcome prejudice and win sympathy and cooperation, is small matter for marvel; but that the daughter of a lowly Negro minister, a seamstress, making her living by her needle, should succeed in doing what Mrs. Joseph has accomplished may be cause for considerable wonder. (*Leadeth*, 2)

Statements of this kind are found in other letters. In praising Gaudet's work among black juveniles, one writer says, "Long before the establishment of the Juvenile court and long before any white woman thought of lending the influence of her presence at the children's trials, Frances Joseph faithfully attended the courts" (*Leadeth*, 8).

These writers earnestly intended to praise Gaudet for her work, especially in the face of her economic circumstances. However, the earnestness of the praise reinforces the discourse of otherness. By measuring Gaudet against a white model, her supporters helped to reinscribe the very discourse that made her efforts so difficult in the first place. In using the wealthy, white Fry as a standard against which to measure the black reformer, Gaudet supporters assumed there existed a natural relationship between social consciousness, morality, and white womanhood, despite Gaudet's impact and explicit challenge to this model.

One white woman went as far as to tell Gaudet that she should have been white. After Gaudet had explained strategies to end the dehumanizing way in which criminals were piled into police vans, the lady responded, "my, you have a fine mind, you ought to be a white woman"

(*Leadeth,* 141). Gaudet recounts her response: "I felt hurt and answered—'I would not insult my God who made me by finding fault with this swarthy skin. He knows what is best and places me where He had need of me, and I am grateful to Him for the opportunity to show the world that I can serve Him well where He had placed me'" (*Leadeth,* 141). By grounding her response in the tenets of Christianity, Gaudet effectively calls attention to the secular basis of the women's position and that of any one who measured her against white women. In the Christian context, God is supreme and omniscient, and everyone else—regardless of race, gender, or class—is spiritually equal to each other but below God. Anyone who measures her against earthly notions of what she should be questions God's will, which in the Christian context is a sin.

Frances Joseph Gaudet's life reveals that she was indeed highly moral, and that her life was centered around religion, or her obligation to God. However, both her active participation in prison reform, education reform, and the education of juvenile delinquents and the social changes brought about by her efforts demand that she not be simply categorized as a moral person concerned primarily with her individual spiritual development. Gaudet continued a tradition of social involvement set forth by other black women preachers such as Jarena Lee and Julia Foote—a tradition that begs for a space for serious consideration of them as active agents for social change. Such a consideration of this tradition will no doubt expand our definitions and understandings of black feminist thought. The way in which religion is used as an agent for social change by black women preachers can also expand our approaches to interpreting and understanding nineteenth-century black literature and life in general as well.

SEVEN

Can I Get a Witness?

THE IMPLICATIONS OF PROPHESYING FOR
AFRICAN AMERICAN LITERARY STUDIES

When Jarena Lee, Julia Foote, Maria Stewart, Frances Gaudet, and other prophesying daughters finished writing their narratives, they actually had created what I call *autometagraphies.* That is, their narratives reveal an understanding of themselves that transcends earthly constructions of their lives and identities. Every aspect of their being was interpreted from a metaphysical vantage point that allowed them to see themselves as prophesying daughters, a perception that would in many ways require them to challenge nineteenth-century notions of who they should be. They saw themselves retrospectively through new-found spiritual lenses. Their writing about their own long and arduous travel excursions, emotionally charged conversion experiences, profound interpretations of the Bible, and undying passion for social change reveals clearly a consciousness that had been formed and informed by their close relationships with and commitments to God—the metaphysical—who had everything to do with all incidents, events, or lack thereof that occurred in their lives. Their lives, works, and self-perceptions are inseparable.

In the preceding chapters, I have delineated how these women's perception of themselves as prophesying daughters shaped what and how they chose to write these autometagraphies. As the discussion has revealed, they used rhetoric around the Pauline conversion experience to dispute mainstream society's distrust of their intellectual, literary, and missionary abilities as writers and preachers. They also likened themselves to Jesus' disciples to justify their travel, which itself altered in various ways the American cultural and spatial landscape. They utilized effectively their own understandings of the Bible to offer alternative readings of scriptures and to legitimate their "aberrant" actions. And, finally, in their texts they used their calling as prophesying daughters to be active agents for social change.

What this reveals is that the act of prophesying offers us insight into the ways in which these black religious women understood and ordered their lives. In their identification of themselves as prophesying daughters, Lee, Foote, Gaudet, and Stewart provide us with clear examples of the use and application of religion and religious perspectives in their lives and writings. I contend that illuminating the complex ways that black women preachers had to (re)negotiate religious belief and conviction in the context of the nineteenth-century's sexist, elitist, and racist climate is one of the primary contributions that these texts make to African American literary experience and literary production.

In light of the above, then, what are the implications of my study for African American literature in general and for African American women's works in particular? In other words, how can this study help expand the ways we critically examine several of their black female contemporaries and predecessors such as Phillis Wheatley, Frances E. W. Harper, Elizabeth Keckley, and Harriet Jacobs, all of whom employed religious discourse and rhetoric throughout their writings? How is the study helpful when we consider that the appropriation of religion and Christian ideas by black women writers and intellectuals cannot be a coincidence? Historically, blacks have had a long and paradoxical relationship with Christian religion in this country.

Furthermore, what about this notion of the women's perception of themselves as people "called" to make a difference? How is that significant to the field of African American literary studies? I begin to address these questions by proposing a theory of prophesying. Before delineating the features of a text that could be said to prophesy, I situate my proposal of a new theory within debates in African American literary studies about where to place or displace theory.

Since the eighties, critics have engaged in interesting and sometimes heated discussions about whether approaches to interpreting African American literature should be theoretical or practical (meaning political). In her seminal essay addressing this issue, Barbara Christian responds to what she calls a "take-over in the literary world" by those who have "changed literary critical language to suit their own purposes" and have consequently "reinvented the meaning of theory." Although she notes that her first impulse in regard to this takeover was to "ignore it," she finds it difficult to do so because the decision to use or overlook theory plays a key role in the lives of scholars and professors. The use or nonuse of theory, Christian argues, determines "whether we were hired or promoted in academic institutions—worse, whether we were heard at all." This condition puts the new generation of critics who study works by people of color in a bind, forcing them into "speaking a language and defining their discussion in terms alien to and opposed to their own needs and orientation." What makes the language foreign, according to Christian, is "its linguistic jargon, its emphasis in quoting the prophets, its tendency towards 'Biblical exegesis,' its refusal even to mention specific works of creative writers, far less contemporary ones, its preoccupation with mechanical analyses of language, graphs, algebraic equations, its gross generalizations about culture." The result of such nonnative language has been a silencing of many critics of color.[1]

In essence, Christian is saying that this "movement to exalt theory" means that those who accept and use it are often seen as serious scholars, and that those who opt not to embrace it are seen as simplistic. Christian herself stresses that she is not antitheory, as some of her critics later charged. Michael Awkward, for example, says that Christian's article "leaves no doubt in the minds of the readers" that she is "against theory." He notes that Christian's discussion does not account for the ways in which uses of the theories she denounces have "indeed deepened our received knowledge of the textual production of black writers." Joining the conversation, Henry Louis Gates admits that Christian's take on the uses of theory can be seen as "an attack on the personal integrity and recent work of critics who opted to utilize it. These critics, he asserts, use theory "because they believe it offers provocative means of discussing the texts of non-hegemonic groups" and also because "theory is viewed by them as useful in the critical analysis of the literary products of 'the other.' "[2]

This debate unfolds in the well-known heated exchange in *New Literary History* (Winter 1987) between Joyce Joyce, Gates, and Houston

1. Barbara Christian, "A Race for Theory," 348, 349, 350.
2. Michael Awkward, "Appropriative Gestures: Theory and Afro-American Literary Criticism," 361; Henry Louis Gates, " 'What's Love Got to Do with It?': Critical Theory, Integrity, and the Black Idiom," 363.

Baker. Despite the unnecessary personal, professional, and intellectual attacks the three scholars hurled at each other in this altercation, the place of theory in African American literary studies centered the debate. Joyce sees the "merger of Negro expression with Euro-American expression" as a simultaneous adoption of "pseudoscientific language" that she deems "distant and sterile." The use of such language, according to Joyce, somehow negates the "blackness" that many writers had worked so hard to define and attain. Gates responds by noting that the use of poststructuralism in no way undermines a black critic's "blackness." He emphasizes that his whole approach as a black critic has been to try "to work through contemporary theories of literature *not* to 'apply' them to black texts, but rather to *transform* by *translating* them into a new rhetorical realm."[3] Baker agrees that there is a need in the development of black literary history to take discussions of black texts to another level by employing other existing theoretical models.

Interestingly, many black feminist critics such as Frances Smith Foster and Deborah McDowell actually agree with Baker to a certain extent, and they themselves encourage a kind of cautious, cross-theoretical approach to interpreting African American literature. My theory of prophesying is situated in this particular camp, which endorses mediation over exclusion. Deborah McDowell, for example, warns that theories should not be used without an awareness of how historical knowledge about literary theory gets created and constructed. McDowell is not against the use of theory, but she is against tendencies to privilege uncritically uses of theory so that critics who embrace and apply it are valorized over those who do not. Offering a similar view, Frances Smith Foster contends that "as literature the productions of African American women may be subjected to the various theoretical perspectives."[4] So while Foster acknowledges that various theoretical models can be used to understand the "amalgam," the "mixture of diverse elements," that make up African American women's texts, one cannot analyze them without

3. Joyce Joyce, "'Who the Cap Fit': Unconsciousness and Unconscionableness in the Criticism of Houston A. Baker, Jr. and Henry Louis Gates, Jr." 339; Gates, "What's Love," 351.

4. Deborah McDowell, "New Directions for Black Feminist Criticism," in *The Changing Same: Black Women's Literature, Criticism, and Theory*; Foster, *Written by Herself*, 15.

acknowledging the "social and historical forces of its times" and how those forces shaped the texts.

My theory of prophesying—which is consistent with views such as McDowell's and Foster's—is based on the clear evidence that the black women preachers here discussed used their critical abilities to challenge the hegemonic use of Christianity without rejecting Christianity itself. Being what Zora Neale Hurston called "appropriative creatures," the women were critically sophisticated enough to discriminate among choices, detecting and sometimes discarding the aspects of Christianity used against them while acknowledging and making use of those that they thought were mentally, spiritually, and physically helpful for them. They did this so often by engaging in what Fiorenza and other biblical scholars call the "hermeneutics of suspicion"—where illegitimate interpretations used for oppressive or hegemonic purposes were considered suspect. That is what I think Foster, McDowell, and others are calling for in regard to the use of theory and other analytical concepts in critical discussions of African American women's works. They are saying that we should not simply dismiss literary theory and its uses, but rather that we should regard with suspicion any tendency to elevate as superior criticisms of texts that use established (European-based) theory and to downgrade the readings of critics who choose not to utilize the more established and popular models.

In light of this discussion, I do think that at this point in the development and criticism of African American literature, there is sufficient room for a theory of prophesying. The possibilities of such a theory—demonstrated in this close examination of the works of four black women preachers—may lead to a more comprehensive view of African American literature. I place my theory of prophesying alongside the important, pioneering efforts already put forth by Houston Baker, Henry Louis Gates, and Barbara Smith. Baker provided the field with a blues theory that allows us to find cultural meaning and theoretical possibilities in the blues song. Gates expanded the analytical possibilities of African American literature by using the trickster figure as a basis for the theory of signifying. Though initially met with serious opposition, Barbara Smith offered lesbian theory as an alternative to understanding African American women's literature in particular.

With the theory of prophesying presented here, I aim to offer an alternative way of interpreting literature with strong religious imagery, themes, and subthemes. After studying the texts of Jarena Lee, Julia Foote, Maria Stewart, and Frances Joseph Gaudet, from which I draw the concept's formative elements, I conclude that under certain conditions a text could be said to prophesy. A text prophesies if in it the world of the Bible is appropriated and recreated in order to offer a critique of current social and political conditions. A text also prophesies if it deconstructs religious ideology used to justify oppressive behavior, replacing it with more liberating counterinterpretations. Finally, a text prophesies if it forces the reader to acknowledge that there are no distinctions between the religious and the secular—if it blurs the supposed boundary between these two binaries so that the reader sees that both interact, with one influencing the other on many levels. While a prophesying text may not exemplify all of these things together, more than one of these features are always at play in it.

Furthermore, the ability of a text to prophesy depends in part on the reader's familiarity with certain Christian concepts and ideals. In other words, there is a presupposition that the reader—in order to fully appreciate the deconstructive power of texts by nineteenth-century and contemporary black women writers who use religious discourse in an attempt to challenge and change society—is at least generally aware of key biblical stories and the significance of discipleship and conversion rhetoric in the Christian context. I am not suggesting that textual prophesying calls for a transhistorical reading of black women's works, but rather that somehow and across history, black women writers from Wheatley to Morrison have managed to manipulate religious discourse in powerful, deconstructive ways. An awareness of these basic categories may open up fascinating possibilities for reading works with religious motifs as sophisticated and complex rather than as simple texts.

But how might one begin to apply this idea of prophesying to other (black women's) texts? We could see that by looking at, for example, Harriet Jacobs's *Incidents in the Life of a Slave Girl*.[5] I have selected *Incidents* to illustrate the concept's applicability because it is a text both widely read and critically analyzed, and one with significant religious undercurrents. In addition, unlike Lee, Foote, and many of her overtly religious

5. Quotations from Harriet Jacobs's *Incidents in the Life of a Slave Girl*. Hereafter citations will be made parenthetically, with the abbreviation *Incidents* followed by the page number.

contemporaries, Jacobs was more secular and is thus unfortunately not necessarily seen as "religious" in the sense that the other women are. Even Harper, because she has written copious works in which she overtly employs religious themes, has been more readily associated with religion. Consequently, my notion of prophesying could easily be applied to several of Harper's works. One could argue that in her essay "Our Greatest Want," for example, Harper's use of the image of Moses to encourage economic, political, and social changes for blacks in the nineteenth century carries serious prophetic implications. Harper draws no lines between the secular and the sacred. She in fact connects the two, suggesting that one always influences the other. By using the image of Moses in this piece, as well as in her narrative poem "Moses: A Story of the Nile," she engages the world of the Bible to make social commentary on the present issue of slavery. The same can be said of how she handles religious discourse in poems, short stories, and novels to expose various ambiguities in the nineteenth-century use of Christianity. Her multi-genre use of religious discourse to critique and try to change the secular makes a strong case for the applicability of the poetics of prophesying not only to Harper's writings but also to *Incidents*.

I mentioned earlier that *Incidents* has been widely criticized and analyzed. Scholars have done excellent work authenticating the veracity of the text, showing how it reconstructs notions of womanhood, how its very publication reveals much about the politics of text production for nineteenth-century black women writers, and how it has transformed many literary conventions (slave narratives, sentimental novels, and autobiography). However, only a few discussions analyze Jacobs's deconstructive use of religious discourse, and hardly any of them associate the text with prophesying. Frances Foster admits that while several scholars have examined Jacobs's text in ways that show its importance to African American literary history, "discussions of generic influences generally have ignored or glossed over the impact of the religious narrative tradition."[6] Foster then very briefly mentions that writers such as Jarena Lee and Angelina Grimke influenced Jacobs with their emphasis on social reform, their advocacy for women's participation in public life, and their belief in the social impact of communities of women working

6. Foster, *Written by Herself*, 97.

for the common good. I extend the important conversation Foster has started by offering a reading of *Incidents* as a prophetic text. In this reading, I establish more specifically the influence of religious discourse on Jacobs's writings.

The prophetic significance of *Incidents* is seen specifically in Jacobs's instructive use of religious discourse to alert white women to their complacency with and complicity in the suffering of black women and also to warn them of the spiritual dangers they face if they do not correct their acquiescent behavior. She begins immediately on the title page, issuing this warning from Isaiah 32:9: "Rise up ye women who are at ease! Hear my voice, ye careless daughters. Give ear to my speech." As the biblical figure Isaiah cautioned against societal complacency with Egyptian slavery, so Jacobs admonishes white women that they are being "careless" in their inaction to help free black women from bondage. She encourages white women to rise up and become politically involved in advocating for change. Jacobs has already taken the initial responsibility for trying to inspire change by writing a text that will allow her to voice her concerns about the conditions of black women in slavery. Seeing her text as prophetic, as one that can be used to invoke social change, she wants white women to "hear her," to "give ear" to her words and hence act accordingly.

Jacobs not only sets the tone for the prophetic use of her text in the title page, but she also—in the hope of inspiring change—continues to strategically invoke scriptures throughout the text as a foundation for offering social critique and for exposing contradictions in the use of Christian principles. For example, after her mistress dies, she learns that she has been bequeathed to her mistress's niece. To comment on what she perceives to be a huge flaw in the logic advanced by Christians to justify holding slaves, Jacobs refers to Mark 12:31—which is considered the second great commandment and golden rule—and to Matthew 7:12, referred to as the law of the prophets. Jacobs writes: "My mistress taught me the precepts of God's Word: 'Thou shalt love thy neighbor,' and 'whatsoever ye would that men should do unto you, do ye even so unto them.' But I was her slave and I suppose she did not recognize me as her neighbor" (*Incidents*, 11). Scripture is deployed again to further criticize white women for not living up to the same principles of Christianity that they themselves taught their slaves. It shows that the women may speak one way about how their fellow believers should be treated, but that they hypocritically act quite differently when those believers are slaves.

Jacobs prophesies even further in her commentary on her second mistress's disturbing ability to watch calmly as slaves were brutally beaten. She writes how Mrs. Flint would "sit in her easy chair and see a woman whipped, till the blood trickled from every stroke of the lash. She was a member of the church; but partaking in the Lord's supper did not seem to put her in a Christian mind" (*Incidents*, 22). Jesus' "last supper" with his disciples is commemorated by Christians in their participation in a similar symbolic "supper" of drinking wine (representing Christ's blood) and eating bread (representing Christ's body). This ritual signifies a symbolic rededication to the principles of Christianity and a recommitment to holy living. That Mrs. Flint could participate in this religious exercise and at the same time endure and even allow such inhumane treatment of slaves or fellow humans speaks volumes of her bigotry and that of the larger slavocracy. Jacobs's prophetic statement in selecting this example is that white women who are "at ease," who participate in the supper and still do no try to change the conditions of slaves, are just as guilty as Mrs. Flint of not living up to Christian principles.

Illustrating the aspect of prophesying that speaks against mistranslation of theology for oppressive ends, Jacobs further criticizes slave masters' tendency to misuse the biblical subject of the curse of Ham as justification for the enslavement of blacks: "They [the slaveholders] seem to satisfy their consciences with the doctrine that God created the Africans to be slaves" (*Incidents*, 39). As do Lee and Foote, Jacobs renders such a reading suspect, detecting that it is put forth in order to maintain the status quo. She is aware that there are "intelligent slaves" like herself who are able to discern the misuse of this scriptural event. Confident in her own conviction, her own understanding of God's will, she states, "what a libel upon the heavenly Father, who 'made of one blood all nations of men!' " (*Incidents*, 39). God himself drew no "racial" distinction between men and women, be they slaves or masters. According to Jacobs, the use of the curse of Ham is actually a blatant misreading of God's divine will. *Incidents* prophesies, therefore, by exposing these oppressive uses of the Bible as flawed and overtly wrong. As do the works of Lee, Foote, Stewart, and Gaudet in similar situations, the narrative replaces such a reading with a counterinterpretation supported by another scriptural statement: "God made all men of one blood."

It must be emphasized that Jacobs was also aware of the internal paradox that slavery posed for slaves who aspired to be Christians. These contradictions surfaced often when the slaves' earthly masters required or expected them to do something that went against their heavenly master's expectations. During a conversation that Jacobs's character Brent has with her brother, William, we see William grappling with this very issue. He realizes the serious tension slaves experience when they are expected to be good in the context of an entire institution that is built upon evil. William confides in his sister, "I try to be good; but what is the use?" (*Incidents*, 19). As had George's master in Brown's *Clotel* and Douglass's in his *Narrative*, William's master constantly attempted to beat and demean him in efforts to undermine his masculinity.

William's master was also deceitful. In one incident, he passes pennies off as silver dollars to an old man and makes William use the fake money to purchase items. Jacobs's character, Linda, advises her brother to abide by the Christian principles of being good and forgiving, but she does so by acknowledging the conflicts she herself experiences when faced with this issue. She notes that "while I advised him to be good and forgiving, I was not unconscious of the beam in my own eye" (*Incidents*, 19). This reference to Matthew 7:3–5 and Luke 6:44–42 provides an example of the discursive inversion of biblical discourse in which prophesying daughters often had to engage. The full text that she references reads: "And why beholdest thou the mote that is in thy brother's eye, but considerest the beam that is in thine eye? Or how wilt thou say to thy brother, let me pull out the mote out of thine eye, and behold, a beam is in thine eye. Thou hypocrite, first cast out the beam out of thine own eye; and then shalt though see clearly to cast out the mote out of thy brother's eye."

Although "the Word" required slaves to be good, the situation of slavery forced them to redefine the parameters of this good. Jacobs notes that "I had not lived fourteen years in slavery for nothing. I have felt, seen, and heard enough, to read the characters, and question the motives of those around me" (*Incidents*, 19). She had attained from experience a deconstructive beam that exposed ambiguities and inconsistencies in the use of Christianity. Jacobs concludes that, "though one of God's most powerless creatures, I resolved never to be conquered" (*Incidents*, 19). She later uses what little power she has over her own body to choose her own lover and have his children rather than accept the advances of her master, Dr. Flint.

Jacobs's narrative use of the Bible to offer correctives to nineteenth-century social injustices against black women is neither ahistorical nor coincidental. The issue of religion and the ideas of Christianity abound in the works of black women writers and intellectuals as diverse as Wheatley, Wilson, Harper, Kelly, and Wells in the nineteenth century to Zora Neale Hurston and Toni Morrison in the twentieth. Perhaps this theory of prophesying offers another possibility for exploring and understanding the contradictions and complexities of this engagement with religion in the literary works of many other black women writers.

This discussion illustrates that despite the rampant uncertainties of life for nineteenth-century blacks, there was one thing of which Jarena Lee, Julia Foote, Frances Joseph Gaudet, Maria Stewart, and other prophesying daughters were certain. They knew for sure that they had been singled out by God and sent out into that volatile world to perform religious acts that would change it. Amazingly, almost two centuries ago, despite the apparently insurmountable challenges that this call presented, they listened to it and responded.

While responding, they often referred to themselves as "humble instruments of God." However, their preaching, their challenging social structures, and their questioning ideologies all reflected and even required a certain amount of arrogance. This spiritual narcissism emanated from another view of themselves (to use Foote's title) as "brands plucked from the fire," and they were so resolute in the conviction that they had emerged tested, tried, and true that they gave a spiritual cold shoulder to the heat they encountered from daily confrontations with racism, sexism, and classism.

Finally, so determined were they to answer their call to God that they felt it necessary to record their activities, views, and philosophies. In doing so, they left evidence of the things seen, done, and changed by them. To borrow a concept from Cornel West, they delivered the prophecy, and in so doing they left rich interpretative possibilities for the field of African American literary studies.

Selected Bibliography

Andrews, William L. "The Novelization of Voice in Early African American Narrative." *PMLA* 105:1 (1990): 23–34.

———. "The Politics of African-American Ministerial Autobiography." In *African-American Christianity: Essays in History,* ed. Paul E. Johnson, 111–33. Berkeley and Los Angeles: University of California Press, 1994.

———. *Sisters of the Spirit: Three Black Women's Autobiographies of the Nineteenth Century.* Bloomington: Indiana University Press, 1986.

———. *To Tell A Free Story: The First Century of Afro-American Autobiography, 1760–1865.* Urbana: University of Illinois Press, 1986.

———. "Toward a Poetics of Afro-American Autobiography." In *Afro-American Literary Studies in the 1990's,* ed. Houston A. Baker Jr. and Patricia Redmond, 78–91. Chicago: University of Chicago Press, 1989.

"The Atlantic Steamships." Advertisement. *Christian Recorder.* June 1862.

Augustine. *The Confessions.* Trans. R. S. Pine-Coffin. New York: Penguin, 1961.

Awkward, Michael. "Appropriative Gestures: Theory and Afro-American Literary Criticism." In *Within the Circle: An Anthology of African American Literary Criticism from the Harlem Renaissance to the Present,* ed. Angelyn Mitchell, 360–67. Durham, N.C.: Duke University Press, 1994.

Bakhtin, M. M. *The Dialogic Imagination.* Austin: University of Texas Press, 1981.

Baker, Houston. *Blues, Ideology, and Afro-American Literature: A Vernacular Theory.* Chicago: University of Chicago Press, 1984.

Barbour, John D. "Character and Characterization in Religious Auto-biography." *Journal of the American Academy of Religion* 55:2 (1987): 307–27.

Beckford, James. "Accounting for Conversion." *British Journal of Sociology* 29:2 (June 1978): 249–62.

Bennett, Anne. *From Woman-Pain to Woman-Vision: Writings in Feminist Theology.* Minneapolis: Fortress Press, 1975.

Bercovitch, Sacvan. *The Puritan Origins of the American Self.* New Haven: Yale University Press, 1975.

Blunt, Alison. *Travel, Gender, and Imperialism: Mary Kingsley and West Africa.* New York: Guilford Press, 1994.

Braude, Ann D. "Spirits Defend the Rights of Women: Spiritualism and Changing Sex Roles in Nineteenth-Century America." In *Women, Religion, and Social Change,* ed. Yvonne Yazbeck Haddad and Ellison Banks Findly, 419–31. Albany: State University of New York Press, 1985.

Brauer, Jerald C. "Conversion: From Puritanism to Revivalism." *Journal of Religion* 58:3 (July 1978): 227–43.

Braxton, Joanne. *Black Women Writing Autobiography: A Tradition within a Tradition.* Philadelphia: Temple University Press, 1989.

Bryan, Violet H. "Frances Joseph Gaudet: Black Philanthropist." *Sage* 3:1 (Spring 1986): 46–49.

Butler, Judith. *Gender Trouble: Feminism and the Subversion of Identity.* New York: Routledge, 1990.

Butterfield, Stephen. *Black Autobiography in America.* Amherst: University of Massachusetts Press, 1974.

Caldwell, Patricia. *The Puritan Conversion Narrative: The Beginnings of American Expression.* New York: Cambridge University Press, 1983.

Cannon, Katie. "The Bible from the Perspective of the Racially and Economically Oppressed." In *Scripture: The Word beyond the Word,* ed. Nancy A. Carter, 35–40. New York: United Methodist Church, 1985.

———. *Black Womanist Ethics.* Atlanta: Scholars Press, 1988.

———. "Slave Ideology and Biblical Interpretation." *Semeia* 4 (1989): 9–23.

Carby, Hazel. *Reconstructing Womanhood: The Emergence of the African-American Woman Novelist.* New York: Oxford University Press, 1989.

Christian, Barbara. "But What Do We Think We're Doing Anyway: The State of Black Feminist Criticism(s) or My Own Version of a Little Bit of History." In *Within the Circle: An Anthology of African American Literary Criticism from the Harlem Renaissance to the Present*, ed. Angelyn Mitchell, 499–514. Durham, N.C.: Duke University Press, 1994.

———. "A Race for Theory." In *Within the Circle: An Anthology of African American Literary Criticism from the Harlem Renaissance to the Present*, ed. Angelyn Mitchell, 348–59. Durham, N.C.: Duke University Press, 1994.

Cohen, Patricia Cline. *A Calculating People: The Spread of Numeracy in Early America*. Chicago: University of Chicago Press, 1972.

Collier-Thomas, Bettye. *Daughters of Thunder: Black Women Preachers and Their Sermons, 1850–1879*. San Francisco: Jossey-Bass, 1998.

Collins, Patricia Hill. *Black Feminist Thought: Knowledge, Consciousness, and the Politics of Empowerment*. Boston: Unwin Hyman, 1990.

Cone, James. *For My People: Black Theology and the Black Church*. New York: Orbis, 1984.

———. *A Theology of Black Liberation*. Philadelphia: Lippincott, 1970.

Connor, Kimberly Rae. *Conversions and Visions in the Writings of African-American Women*. Knoxville: University of Tennessee Press, 1994.

Cooper, Anna Julia Haywood. *A Voice from the South, by a Black Woman of the South*. 1892. Reprint, Westport, Conn.: Greenwood Press, 1976.

Daly, Robert. "Puritan Poetic." In *Early American Literature: A Collection of Critical Essays,* ed. Michael Gilmore. Englewood Cliffs, N.J.: Prentice Hall, 1980.

Davidman, Lynn, and Arthur Griel. "Gender and the Experience of Conversion; The Case of 'Returners' to Modern Orthodox Judaism." In *Gender and Religion,* ed. William Swatos Jr., 105–12. New Brunswick, N.J.: Transaction, 1994.

Davis, Angela. *Women, Race, and Class*. New York: Vintage, 1983.

Davis, Mary Kemp. *Nat Turner before the Bar of Judgment: Fictional Treatments of the Southampton Slave Insurrection*. Baton Rouge: Louisiana State University Press, 1999.

Dayton, Donald. Preface to *Holiness Tracts Defending the Ministry of Women*. New York: Garland, 1985.

Detweiler, Frederick. *The Negro Press in the United States.* Chicago: University of Chicago Press, 1922.

Dodson, Jualyne. "Nineteenth-Century A.M.E. Preaching Women: Cutting Edge of Women's Inclusion in Church Polity." In *Women in New Worlds: Historical Perspectives on the Wesleyan Tradition,* edited by Hilah F. Thomas, Rosemary Skinner Keller, and Louise L. Queen, 276–79. Nashville: Abingdon Press, 1981.

———. "Power and Surrogate Leadership: Black Women and Organized Religion." *Sage* 5:2 (Fall 1988): 37–42.

Dodson, Jualyne E., and Cheryl Townsend Gilkes. "Something Within: Social Change and Collective Endurance in the Sacred World of Black Christian Women." In *Women and Religion in America,* Vol. 3, *1900–1968,* ed. Rosemary Radford Ruether and Rosemary Skinner Keller, 80–130. San Francisco: Harper and Row, 1986.

Dorsey, Peter. *Sacred Estrangement: The Rhetoric of Conversion in Modern American Autobiography.* University Park: Pennsylvania State University Press, 1993.

Douglas, Ann. *The Feminization of American Culture.* New York: Knopf, 1977.

Douglas, Mary. *Purity and Danger: An Analysis of Concepts of Pollution and Taboo.* London: Routledge and Kegan Paul, 1978.

Douglass, Frederick. *Narrative of the Life of Frederick Douglass, An American Slave, Written by Himself.* Ed. William Andrews and William S. McFeely. New York: W. W. Norton, 1997.

duCille, Ann. *Skin Trade.* Cambridge: Harvard University Press, 1996.

Epstein, Barbara. *The Politics of Domesticity: Women, Evangelism, and Temperance in Nineteenth-Century America.* Middletown, Conn.: Wesleyan University Press, 1981.

Evans, James H., Jr. *Spiritual Empowerment in Afro-American Literature: Frederick Douglass, Rebecca Jackson, Booker T. Washington, Toni Morrison.* Lewiston, N.Y.: Edwin Meller Press, 1983.

"A Fact for Travellers." Announcement. *Christian Reader.* June 6, 1855.

Felder, Cain Hope. Introduction to *Stony the Road We Trod: African American Biblical Interpretation.*, ed. Cain Hope Felder, 1–14. Minneapolis: Fortress Press, 1991.

———. *Troubling Biblical Waters: Race, Class, and Family.* Mary Knoll, N.Y.: Orbis, 1989.

Fitzgerald, Maureen. "The Religious Is Personal Is Political." Foreword to *The Woman's Bible,* by Elizabeth Cady Stanton. Boston: Northeastern University Press, 1993.

Foote, Julia. *A Brand Plucked from the Fire: An Autobiographical Sketch.* 1886. Reprinted in *Spiritual Narratives,* ed. Henry Louis Gates. New York: Oxford University Press, 1988.

Fordham, Monroe. *Major Themes in Northern Black Religious Thought, 1800–1860.* New York: Exposition Press, 1975.

Foster, Frances Smith. "Adding Color and Contour to Early American Self-Portraitures: Autobiographical Writings of Afro-American Women." In *Conjuring: Black Women's Fiction and Literary Tradition,* ed. Marjorie Pryse and Hortense Spillers. Bloomington: Indiana University Press, 1985.

———. "African-American Progress-Report Autobiographies." In *Redefining American Literary History,* ed. Lavonne Brown Ruoff and Jerry W. Ward Jr., 270–83. New York: Modern Language Association, 1990.

———. "Autobiography after Emancipation: The Example of Elizabeth Keckley." In *Multicultural Autobiography: American Lives,* ed. James Robert Payne, 32–63. Knoxville: University of Tennessee Press, 1992.

———. Introduction to *Minnie's Sacrifice, Sowing and Reaping, Trial and Triumph: Three Rediscovered Novels by Frances E. W. Harper.* Boston: Beacon Press, 1994.

———. *Witnessing Slavery: The Development of Ante-bellum Slave Narratives.* 2d ed. Madison: University of Wisconsin Press, 1994.

———. *Written by Herself: Literary Production by African American Women, 1746–1892.* Bloomington: Indiana University Press, 1993.

Foster, Frances, and Chanta M. Haywood. "Christian Recordings: Afro-Protestantism, Its Press, and the Production of African American Literature." *Religion and Literature* 27:1 (Spring 1995): 15–35.

Foster, Shirley. *Across New Worlds: Nineteenth-Century Women Travellers and Their Writings.* Hertfordshire: Harvester Wheatsheaf, 1990.

Gates, Henry Louis. *The Signifying Monkey: A Theory of Afro-American Literary Criticism.* New York: Oxford University Press, 1988.

———. " 'What's Love Got to Do with It?': Critical Theory, Integrity, and the Black Idiom." *New Literary History* 18:2 (Winter 1987): 345–62.

Gaudet, Frances. *He Leadeth Me.* 1913. Reprint, ed. Henry Louis Gates, New York: Oxford University Press, 1996.

Giddings, Paula. *When and Where I Enter: The Impact of Black Women on Race and Sex in America.* New York: William Morrow, 1984.

Gilkes, Cheryl Townsend. "The Politics of 'Silence': Dual-Sex Political Systems and Women's Traditions of Conflict in African-American Religion." In *African American Christianity: Essays in History,* ed. Paul E. Johnson, 80–110. Berkeley and Los Angeles: University of California Press, 1994.

Grant, Jacqueline. *White Women's and Black Women's Jesus: Feminist Christology and Womanist Response.* Atlanta: Scholars Press, 1989.

———. "Womanist Theology: Black Women's Experience as a Source for Doing Theology, with Special Reference to Christology." In *African American Religious Studies: An Interdisciplinary Anthology,* ed. Gayraud Wilmore. Durham, N.C.: Duke University Press, 1989.

Griffin, Charles. "The Rhetoric of Form in Conversion Narratives." *Quarterly Journal of Speech* 76:2 (May 1990): 152–63.

Gruesse, John. "Afro-American Travel Literature and Africanist Discourse." *Black American Literature Forum* 24:1 (Spring 1990): 5–20.

Haddad, Yvonne, and Ellison Banks Findly, eds. *Women, Religion, and Social Change.* Albany: State University of New York Press, 1985.

Hamilton, Charles. *The Black Preacher in America.* New York: William Morrow, 1972.

Hampson, Daphne. *Theology and Feminism.* Cambridge: Basil Blackwell, 1990.

Harpham, Geoffrey Galt. "Conversion and the Language of Autobiography." In *Studies in Autobiography,* ed. James Onley, 42–50. New York: Oxford University Press, 1988.

Haywood, Chanta. "The Christian Recorder." In *The Oxford Companion to African American Literature,* ed. William Andrews, Frances Smith Foster, and Trudier Harris. New York: Oxford University Press, 1997.

———. "Prophesying Daughters: Nineteenth-Century Black Religious Women, the Bible, and Black Literary History." In *African Americans and the Bible: Sacred Texts and Social Textures,* ed. Vincent Wimbush, 355–66. New York: Continuum, 2000.

Hefner, Robert. Introduction to *Conversion to Christianity: Historical and Anthropological Perspectives on a Great Transformation,* 3–44. Berkeley and Los Angeles: University of California Press, 1990.

Henderson, Mae. "Speaking in Tongues: Dialogics, Dialectics, and the Black Woman Writer's Literary Tradition." In *Reading Black, Reading Feminist: A Critical Anthology,* 116–42. New York: Meridian, 1990.

Higginbotham, Evelyn. *Righteous Discontent: The Women's Movement in the Black Baptist Church, 1880–1920.* Cambridge: Harvard University Press, 1993.

Hodges, Graham Russell. Introduction to *Black Itinerants of the Gospel: The Narratives of John Jea and George White.* Madison: Madison House, 1993.

hooks, bell. *Yearning: Race, Gender, and Cultural Politics.* Boston: South End Press, 1990.

Horton, James Oliver. *Free People of Color: Inside the African American Community.* Washington, D.C.: Smithsonian Institution Press, 1993.

Houchins, Sue. Introduction to *Spiritual Narratives,* ed. Henry Louis Gates. New York: Oxford University Press, 1988.

Hubbard, Dolan. *The Sermon and the African American Literary Imagination.* Columbia: University of Missouri Press, 1994.

Humez, Jean. " 'My Spirit Eye': Some Functions of Spiritual and Visionary Experience in the Lives of Five Black Women Preachers, 1810–1880." In *Women and the Structure of Society,* ed. Barbara J. Harris and Jo Ann K. McNamara, 129–42. Durham, N.C.: Duke University Press, 1984.

Humez, Jean, ed. *Gifts of Power: The Writings of Rebecca Jackson, Black Visionary, Shaker Eldress.* Amherst: University of Massachusetts Press, 1981.

Hutton, Frankie. *The Early Black Press in America, 1827–1860.* Westport, Conn.: Greenwood Press, 1993.

Iser, Wolfgang. *The Implied Reader.* Baltimore: John Hopkins University Press, 1974.

Jacobs, Harriet. *Incidents in the Life of a Slave Girl.* New York: Oxford University Press, 1988.

Jobling, David. "Writing the Wrongs of the World: The Deconstruction of the Biblical Text in the Context of Liberation Theologies." *Semeia* 51 (1990): 81–117.

Johnson, Charles H. Introduction to *God Struck Me Dead: Religious Conversion Experiences and Autobiographies of Ex-Slaves,* ed. Clifton H. Johnson. Philadelphia: Pilgrim Press, 1969.

Johnston, Robert K. "Biblical Authority and Interpretation: The Test Case of Women's Role in the Church and Home Updated." In *Women, Authority, and the Bible,* ed. Alvera Mickelsen, 30–41. Downers Groves, Ill.: InterVarsity Press, 1986.

Joyce, Joyce. "The Black Canon: Reconstructing Black American Literary Criticism." *New Literary History* 18:2 (Winter 1987): 335–44.

———. " 'Who the Cap Fit': Unconsciousness and Unconscionableness in the Criticism of Houston A. Baker, Jr. and Henry Louis Gates, Jr." *New Literary History* 18:2 (Winter 1987): 371–84.

Keckley, Elizabeth. *Behind the Scenes: or Thirty Years a Slave and Four Years in the White House.* New York: Oxford University Press, 1988.

Kimball, Gayle. "From Motherhood to Sisterhood: The Search for Female Religious Imagery in Nineteenth and Twentieth Century Theology." In *Beyond Androcentrism: New Essays on Women and Religion,* ed. Rita M. Gross, 259–68. Missoula, Mont.: Scholars Press, 1977.

Krueger, Christine L. *The Reader's Repentance: Women Preachers, Women Writers and Nineteenth-Century Social Discourse.* Chicago: University of Chicago Press, 1992.

Lebra, Taki. "Religious Conversion as a Breakthrough for Transculturation." *Journal for the Scientific Study of Religion* 9:3 (Fall 1970): 181–96.

Lee, Jarena. *The Religious Experience and Journal of Mrs. Jarena Lee: Giving an Account of Her Call to Preach the Gospel.* 1849. Reprinted in *Spiritual Narratives,* ed. Henry Louis Gates. New York: Oxford University Press, 1988.

Lerner, Gerda, ed. *Black Women in White America: A Documentary History.* New York: Vintage, 1972.

Lincoln, C. Eric. "The Development of Black Religion in America." In *African American Religious Studies: An Interdisciplinary Anthology,* ed. Gayraud Wilmore. Durham, N.C.: Duke University Press, 1989.

Lincoln, C. Eric, and Lawrence H. Mamiya. *The Black Church in the African American Experience.* Durham, N.C.: Duke University Press, 1990.

Lofland, John, and Norman Skonovd. "Conversion Motifs." *Journal for the Scientific Study of Religion* 20:4 (December 1981): 373–85.

Long, Theodore, and Jeffery Hadden. "Religious Conversion and the Concept of Socialization." *Journal of the Scientific Study of Religion* 22:1 (March 1983): 1–14.

MacHaffie, Barbara. *Her Story: Women in Christian Tradition.* Philadelphia: Fortress Press, 1986.

Makethan, Lucinda. "From Fugitive Slave to Man of Letters: The Conversation of Frederick Douglass." *Journal of Narrative Technique* 16:1 (Winter 1986): 55–71.

Marsden, George M. "Everyone One's Own Interpreter? The Bible, Science, and Authority in Mid-Nineteenth-Century America." In *The Bible in America: Essays in Cultural History,* ed. Nathan Hatch and Mark Noll. New York: Oxford University Press, 1982.

Mason, Julian, Jr., ed. *The Poems of Phillis Wheatley.* Chapel Hill: University of North Carolina Press, 1989.

Mason, Mary. "Travel as Metaphor and Reality in Afro-American Women's Autobiography, 1850–1972." *Black American Literature Forum* 24:2 (Fall 1990): 337–56.

Mather, Frank Lincoln, ed. *Who's Who in the Colored Race: A General Biographical Dictionary of Men and Women of African Descent.* Vol. 1. 1915. Reprint, Detroit: Gale Research Co., 1976.

McDowell, Deborah. *The Changing Same: Black Women's Literature, Criticism, and Theory.* Bloomington: Indiana University Press, 1995.

Mills, Sara. *Discourses of Differences: An Analysis of Women's Travel Writing and Colonialism.* New York: Routledge, 1991.

Mol, Hans. *Identity and Religion: A Sketch for a New Social Scientific Theory of Religion.* New York: Free Press, 1977.

Montgomery, Maxine Lavon. *The Apocalypse in African American Fiction.* Gainesville: University Press of Florida, 1996.

Moody, Joycelyn. "On the Road with God: Travel and Quest in Early Nineteenth-Century African American Holy Women's Narratives." *Religion and Literature* 27:1 (Spring 1995): 35–51.

———. *Sentimental Confessions: Spiritual Narratives of Nineteenth-*

Century African American Women. Athens: University of Georgia Press, 2001.

Morrison, Toni. "Unspeakable Things Unspoken: The Afro-American Presence in American Literature." In *Within the Circle: An Anthology of African American Literary Criticism from the Harlem Renaissance to the Present,* ed. Angelyn Mitchell, 368–97. Durham, N.C.: Duke University Press, 1994.

Mosala, Itumeleng J. *Biblical Hermeneutics and Black Theology in South Africa.* Grand Rapids, Mich.: William B. Eerdmans, 1989.

Moses, Wilson. *Black Messiahs and Uncle Toms: Social And Literary Manipulations of a Religious Myth.* Rev. ed. University Park: Pennsylvania State University Press, 1993.

———. "The Poetic of Ethiopianism: W.E.B. DuBois and Literary Black Nationalism." *American Literature* 47:3 (1975): 411–26.

Neverdon-Morton, Cynthia. *Afro-American Women of the South and the Advancement of the Race, 1895–1925.* Knoxville: University of Tennessee Press, 1989.

Nichols, Ashton. "Silencing the Other: Discourse of Domination in Nineteenth-Century Exploration Narratives." *Nineteenth-Century Studies* 3 (1989): 1–22.

Nicole, Roger. "Biblical Authority and Feminist Aspirations." In *Women, Authority and the Bible,* ed. Alvera Mickelsen, 43–50. Downers Grove, Ill.: InterVarsity Press, 1986.

Olney, James. " 'I Was Born': Slave Narratives, Their Status as Autobiography and as Literature." In *The Slave's Narrative: Texts and Contexts,* ed. Charles T. Davis and Henry Louis Gates Jr., 148–75. New York: Oxford University Press, 1985.

Overton, Betty J. "Black Women Preachers: A Literary View." *Southern Quarterly* 23:3 (Spring 1995): 157–66.

Painter, Nell Irvin. "Representing Truth: Sojourner Truth's Knowing and Becoming Known." *Journal of American History* 81:2 (September 1994): 461–92.

———. *Sojourner Truth: A Life, A Symbol.* New York: W. W. Norton, 1996.

Pearce, Roy Harvey. *Savagism and Civilization: A Study of the Indian in the American Mind.* Baltimore: John Hopkins University Press, 1953.

Perkins, A. E., ed. *Who's Who in Colored Louisiana: Brief Sketches of History and Biography.* Baton Rouge: Louisiana State University Press, 1930.

Peterson, Carla. *Doers of the Word: African American Women Speakers and Writers in the North, 1830–1880.* New York: Oxford University Press, 1995.

Pinnock, Clark H. "Bibilical Authority and the Issues in Question." In *Women, Authority and the Bible,* ed. Alvera Mickelson, 51–68. Downers Grove, Ill.: InterVarsity Press, 1986.

Pratt, James Bissett. *The Religious Consciousness: A Psychological Study.* New York: Macmillan, 1946.

Pratt, Mary Louise. *Imperial Eyes: Travel Writing and Transculturalism.* New York: Routledge, 1992.

Proctor, William, and Priscilla Proctor. *Women in the Pulpit: Is God an Equal Opportunity Employer?* Garden City, N.Y.: Doubleday, 1976.

Proudfoot, Wayne. *Religious Experience.* Berkeley and Los Angeles: University of California Press, 1985.

Raboteau, Albert. "African-Americans, Exodus, and the American Israel." In *African American Christianity: Essays in History,* ed. Paul E. Johnson, 1–17. Berkeley and Los Angeles: University of California Press, 1994.

———. Introduction to *God Struck Me Dead: Religious Conversion Experiences and Autobiographies of Ex-Slaves.* 2d ed. Philadelphia: Pilgrim Press, 1993.

———. *Slave Religion: The "Invisible Institution" in the Antebellum South.* New York: Oxford University Press, 1978.

Richardson, Marilyn. *Maria Stewart, America's First Black Woman Political Writer: Essays and Speeches.* Bloomington: Indiana University Press, 1987.

Ruether, Rosemary Radford, and Rosemary Skinner Keller, eds. *Women and Religion in America.* Vol. 2, *1900–1968.* San Francisco: Harper and Row, 1986.

Ryan, Mary. *Cradle of the Middle Class: The Family in Oneida County, New York, 1790–1865.* New York: Cambridge University Press, 1981.

"Safe Travelling." Announcement. *Christian Recorder.* February 9, 1861.

Sanders, Cheryl. "The Woman as Preacher." In *African American Studies: An Interdisciplinary Anthology,* ed. Gayraud Wilmore, 372–91. Durham, N.C.: Duke University Press, 1989.

Sarbin, Theodore. "Place Identity as a Component of Self: An Addendum." *Journal of Environmental Psychology* 3 (1983): 337–42.

Schriber, Mary Suzanne, ed. *Telling Travels: Selected Writings by Nineteenth-Century American Women Abroad.* DeKalb: Northern Illinois University Press, 1995.

———. *Writing Home: American Women Abroad, 1830–1920.* Charlottesville: University Press of Virginia, 1997.

Shea, Daniel B., Jr. *Spiritual Autobiography in Early America.* Princeton, N.J.: Princeton University Press, 1968.

Shockley, Ann Allen. Introduction to *Afro-American Women Writers, 1746–1933: An Anthology and Critical Guide.* Boston: G. K. Hall, 1988.

Sigourney, Lydia H. "Home." *Christian Recorder.* January 26, 1861.

Smith, Barbara. "Toward a Black Feminist Criticism." In *Within the Circle: An Anthology of African American Literary Criticism from the Harlem Renaissance to the Present,* ed. Angelyn Mitchell, 410–27. Durham, N.C.: Duke University Press, 1994.

Smith, Sidonie. *A Poetics of Women's Autobiography.* Bloomington: Indiana University Press, 1987.

———. *Where I'm Bound: Patterns of Slavery and Freedom in Black American Autobiography.* Westport, Conn.: Greenwood Press, 1974.

Smith, Theophus. *Conjuring Culture: Biblical Formations of Black America.* New York: Oxford University Press, 1994.

Smith, Valerie. "Gender and Afro-Americanist Literary Theory and Criticism." In *Within the Circle: An Anthology of African American Literary Criticism from the Harlem Renaissance to the Present,* ed. Angelyn Mitchell, 482–89. Durham, N.C.: Duke University Press, 1994.

Snow, David, and Richard Machalek. "The Convert as a Social Type." In *Sociological Theory* 1 (1983): 259–89.

Sobel, Mechal. *Trabelin' On: The Slave Journey to an Afro-Baptist Faith.* Westport, Conn.: Greenwood Press, 1979.

Sollors, Werner. *Beyond Ethnicity: Consent and Descent in American Culture.* New York: Oxford University Press, 1986.

Stanton, Elizabeth Cady. *The Woman's Bible.* Boston: Northeastern University Press, 1993.

Staples, Clifford L., and Armand L. Mauss. "Conversion or Commitment?: A Reassessment of the Snow and Machalek Approach to the Study of Conversion." *Journal for the Scientific Study of Religion* 26:2 (June 1987): 133–47.

Stepto, Robert B. "Distrust of the Reader in Afro-American Narratives." In *Reconstructing American Literary History,* ed. Sacvan Bercovitch. Cambridge: Harvard University Press, 1986.

———. *From Behind the Veil: A Study of Afro-American Narrative.* Urbana: University of Illinois Press, 1979.

Sterling, Dorothy, ed. *We Are Your Sisters: Black Women in the Nineteenth Century.* New York: Norton, 1984.

Stewart, Maria. *The Productions of Mrs. Maria Stewart.* 1835. Reprinted in *Spiritual Narratives,* ed. Henry Louis Gates. New York: Oxford University Press, 1988.

Straus, Roger A. "Religious Conversion as a Personal and Collective Accomplishment." *Sociological Analysis* 40:2 (Summer 1979): 158–65.

Thomas, Hilah F., and Rosemary Skinner Keller, eds. *Women in New Worlds.* Nashville: Parthenon Press, 1981.

Thompkins, Jane. *Sensational Designs: The Cultural Work of American Fiction.* New York: Oxford, 1985.

Thompkins, Jane, ed. *Reader-Response Criticism: From Formalism to Post-Structuralism.* Baltimore: John Hopkins University Press, 1980.

Thurman, Howard. *Jesus and the Disinherited.* Boston: Beacon Press, 1996.

"To Southern Travellers." Announcement. *Christian Recorder.* February 23, 1861.

Travisano, Richard. "Alternation and Conversion as Qualitatively Different Transformation." In *Social Psychology through Symbolic Interaction,* ed. G. P. Stone and H. A. Faberman. Waltham, Mass.: Ginn-Blaisell, 1970.

Tucker, David M. *Black Pastors and Leaders: Memphis, 1819–1972.* Memphis: Memphis State University Press, 1975.

Washington, Mary Helen. "'The Darkened Spiritual Eye Restored': Notes toward a Literary History of Black Women." In *Within the Circle: An Anthology of African American Literary Criticism from the Harlem Renaissance to the Present,* ed. Angelyn Mitchell, 428–42. Durham, N.C.: Duke University Press, 1994.

Weber, Alfred, Beth L. Lueck, and Dennis Berthold. *Hawthorne's American Travel Sketches.* Hanover, N.H.: University Press of New England, 1989.

Weems, Renita. "Reading Her Way through the Struggle: African American Women and the Bible." In *Stony the Road We Trod: African American Biblical Interpretation,* ed. by Cain Hope Felder, 57–77. Minneapolis: Fortress Press, 1991.

Welter, Barbara. *Dimity Convictions: The American Woman in the Nineteenth Century.* Athens: Ohio University Press, 1976.

Wesley, Marilyn. *Secret Journeys: The Trope of Women's Travel in American Literature.* Albany: State University of New York Press, 1997.

West, Cornel. *The Cornel West Reader.* New York: Basis *Civitas* Books, 1999.

Wheatley, Phillis. *The Poems of Phillis Wheatley.* Ed. Julian Mason Jr. Chapel Hill: University of North Carolina Press, 1989.

Williams, Delores. *Sisters in the Wilderness: The Challenge of Womanist God-Talk.* New York: Orbis, 1993.

———. "Women as Makers of Literature." In *Women's Spirit Bonding,* ed. Janet Kalven, 139–45. New York: Pilgrim Press, 1984.

Wilmore, Gayraud, ed. *African American Religious Studies: An Interdisciplinary Anthology.* Durham, N.C.: Duke University Press, 1989.

———. *Black Religion and Black Radicalism.* Garden City, N.Y.: Doubleday, 1972.

Wimbush, Vincent L., ed. *African Americans and the Bible: Sacred Texts and Social Textures.* New York: Continuum Press, 2000.

———."The Bible and African Americans: An Outline of an Interpretative History." In *Stony the Road We Trod: African American Biblical Interpretation,* ed. Cain Hope Felder, 81–88. Minneapolis: Fortress Press, 1991.

———. "Biblical Historical Study as Liberation: Toward an Afro-Christian Hermeneutic." In *African American Religious Studies: An Interdisciplinary Anthology,* ed. Gayraud Wilmore, 140–53. Durham, N.C.: Duke University Press, 1989.

———. "Historical/Cultural Criticism as Liberation: A Proposal for an African American Biblical Hermeneutic." *Semeia* 47 (1989): 43–55.

"Woman and Home." *Christian Recorder.* June 8, 1961.

Wood, Peter. Afterword to *Conversion to Christianity: Historical and An-thropological Perspectives on a Great Transformation,* ed. Robert Hefner, 305–21. Berkeley and Los Angeles: University of California Press, 1990.

Woods, James. "In the Eye of the Beholder: Slavery in the Travel Accounts of the Old South, 1790–1860." *Southern Studies: An Interdisciplinary Journal of the South* 1:1 (Spring 1990): 32–59.

Young, Ida. "Keeping Truth on My Side: Maria Stewart." In *Black Lives: Essays in African American Biogrpahy,* ed. James L. Conyers Jr., 117–28. New York: M. E. Sharpe, 1999.

Zikmund, Barbara Brown. "Biblical Arguments and Women's Place in the Church." In *The Bible and Social Reform,* ed. Ernest R. Sandeen. Chiko, Calif.: Scholars Press for the Society for Biblical Literature, 1982.

Index

African American literature, 65, 117;
autobiographies in, 16, 19–20, 22, 37,
96–97; black women preachers' narratives
in, 16–17, 19, 21, 33, 101, 112, 121;
black women's, 19, 27–28, 91; challenges
to social mores in, 97, 110; conversion
narratives in, 31, 35, 39–40; dialogism
in, 27, 29; letters of authentication in,
37–38, 47–50; narrative techniques in,
18, 24, 47–50; practical vs. theoretical
interpretations of, 112–15; religion in,
22, 24, 112, 116–17; response to reader
mistrust in, 35, 39–40, 47–49; slave
narratives in, 47–49; spiritual narratives
in, 24–25; split between religious and
secular, 23–26; theory of prophesying in,
22, 115–16
African Americans, 59, 59n14, 87; and the
Bible, 75–79, 87; biblical Christianity of,
22–23, 112; conditions of, 11–12, 91,
106; education for, 106–7; institutions
of excluding women, 74, 90, 107; as
prisoners, 10–11, 13; social issues
affecting, 97–98; travel during era of
slavery, 54–56; treated as spiritually
inferior, 2, 7, 75–76, 98–100; using
typological "gyn"esis, 81–82
African Methodist Episcopal (A.M.E.)
Church, 2, 10, 23n14, 54; and women's
roles, 12, 61, 94
African Methodist Episcopal (A.M.E.) Zion,
12–13
Afterlife: effects of belief in, 23–24
Allen, Richard, 23n14, 54; and Lee, 3, 43–44,
62; and women's call to preach, 2–3
Ananias: in Paul's conversion, 41, 43
Andrews, William, 16, 22, 34, 57; on African
American autobiographies, 19, 98;
neglecting role of black women preachers
in social change, 93–94
Anthony, Susan B., 28
Apostolic travel, 111; difficulties of, 51–52,

54, 56, 58, 66–69, 101–2; and gender
expectations, 59–60, 62–66; as marker of
Christianity, 20, 31–32; motivation for,
53–55, 57–58; "othering" for conversion
in, 69–71; Paul's, 42; range of, 52, 64–65
Assimilation, 98
Autobiographies/journals, 42, 76; addressing
reader distrust in, 36–38, 111; African
American, 19–20, 22; of black women
preachers, 16, 111–12; of Foote, 7, 9,
49, 97, 116; of Gaudet, 11, 30, 97, 103,
116; of Lee, 3, 24, 30, 49, 94, 96–98,
116; letters of attestation with, 103;
letters of authentication with, 47–50; and
prophesying, 30, 116; slave narratives as,
47–49; social import of, 93, 97, 102–3;
of Stewart, 97–98, 116; as testimonials,
36–37
Autometagraphies, 111
Awkward, Michael, 113

Baker, Houston, 113–15
Bakhtin, M. M., 18, 26. *See also* Dialogism
Baldwin, Albert, 105
Baldwin, James, 25
Baptist Church: women's roles in, 14, 92
Beckford, James, 36
Beloved (Morrison), 56n8
Bethune, Mary McLeod, 91
Bible, 19, 35; African Americans' choice
of passages from, 78–79, 86–87; black
women preachers' uses of, 77–82;
gender ideology in, 20, 45–47, 74–75;
identification with, 87–88; race ideology
in, 75–76; used to justify opposition to
women preaching, 73–74, 76; used to
justify women's preaching, 14–15, 17–18,
82–83; uses of, 77–79, 88, 102–3, 118–21;
women's roles in, 81–85, 88. *See also*
Biblical interpretations
Biblical interpretations, 20, 32, 75;
alternative, 76–77, 81, 88–89; in

About the Author

Chanta M. Haywood currently serves as the Vice President for Institutional Advancement at Albany State University, where she is the chief fundraiser officer for the school. She completed her doctoral and master's studies in American literature from the University of California at San Diego and her undergraduate education in English from Florida A&M University. A scholar, grant writer, reviewer, and administrator, Haywood has over 20 years of academic professional experience in three university systems (Florida, North Carolina, and Georgia), having worked in different capacities including graduate dean, associate provost for both academic affairs and research, vice president, and full professor. Dr. Haywood was appointed by U.S. Secretary of Education Arne Duncan to serve on the Jacob K. Javits Fellowship Board, which she chaired. Her current academic research interests include literature for children in the black press before the Civil War. She is interested in writing college preparation and success texts as well as inspirational books for children and adolescents.